BIOGRAPHY of

"RUTH with the TRUTH"

WARDELL

Missionary to the Jewish People

BIOGRAPHY of

"RUTH with the TRUTH"

WARDELL

Missionary to the Jewish People
from 1946 to the present

Spiritual "Mom" of
Dr. Arnold G. Fruchtenbaum

Written by

Ruth Wardell and Jeffrey Gutterman

Biography of "RUTH with the TRUTH" Wardell: Missionary to the Jewish People

Copyright © 2011 by Ruth Wardell and Jeffrey Gutterman

ISBN: 978-1-935174-08-0

Library of Congress Control Number: 2011900381

BIO018000 Biography & Autobiography: Religious

BIO002000 Religion: Messianic Judaism

REL030510 Religion – Evangelism – Personal Witnessing

Printed in the United States of America

Cover design by Olivier J. Melnick
www.oliviermelnick.com

Published by:

11926 Radium Street
P.O. Box 792507
San Antonio, TX
www.Ariel.org

❧ Friends of Ruth through the Years ❧

Dr. Paul Lee Tan—Paul Tan Prophetic Ministries, Inc. (PTPM). "We feel that God has brought Ruth to our lives for a purpose. That purpose is to encourage me and my family in Christian service and to continue helping in the Chinese work in Dallas, as God enables. 'Ruth with the Truth' will always be a part of our family's spiritual heritage. We all thank God for raising up such an effective and humble servant of His in these Last Days."

Dr. Michael Rydelnik—Moody Bible Institute- Professor of Jewish Studies. "Ruth was always taking us on trips. We would go canoeing in New Jersey. Ruth would load up two vans with kids and head out. She would drive the van down the highway with her knees while her hands were in the air as she led the group in a song. We didn't need the radio. We would just sing songs about Jesus. My earliest memories of Ruth were of a person who was bold, yet tolerant and understanding.

Dr. Arnold Fruchtenbaum—Director of Ariel Ministries. "Ruth Wardell first came knocking on my family's door in 1957 when I was living on Blake Avenue in the Van Sicklen section of Brooklyn, New York. She came in with a card in her hand that had been filled out about six years earlier. Miss Wardell's organization was a Jewish Christian group. In my mind, one was either a Jew or a Christian. How could one be both? I concluded that any Jew that believed in Christ had to be suffering from schizophrenia. Since I was having trouble resolving this contradiction I became angry." Arnold was determined to prove her wrong about Jesus being the Jewish Messiah.

Dr. Daniel Goldberg—International Ministires Representative for Chosen People Ministries. "Of all of the missionaries under my supervision in the California area of the Western District, Ruth excelled as a self-starter and exhibited great ability as a leader in winning many followers. She truly utilized her God-given talents as an excellent Bible teacher and friend to the friendless."

Dr. Mitch Glaser—President of Chosen People Ministries. "I knew Ruth as a person who always rose above it all. She never had a bad word about anybody. She was always positive and encouraging. Ruth was an example during those years of someone who was faithful and someone whom I admired greatly."

Moishe Rosen—Founder of Jews For Jesus. "I met Ruth Wardell in 1954 when she was with American Board of Missions to the Jews. Many teens she worked with looked to her for leadership well into their adult lives. I remember Ruth always set a good example."

DEDICATION

I would like to dedicate this book,
first and foremost to

JESUS THE MESSIAH

Who is my
lifetime, precious and always Friend

and also to

ARNOLD FRUCHTENBAUM

who has taught me
the Scriptures from a Jewish perspective,
who has greatly enhanced
my spiritual life, and
who has given me much joy and
excitement in learning God's Word.

PREFACE

In the course of writing my autobiography, I have been abundantly blessed by those who wrote stories, anecdotes, and memories for the book. I would like to thank all those who shared some interesting times they knew from the past. These stories have given me a wonderful opportunity to look back and see how God, in His mercy, has blessed me over these many years, making my life come together with greater meaning. I would like you to know that, without the Lord Jesus in my life, none of these things would have been possible. To Him be all of the praise for allowing me the privilege of serving Him.

I would like to thank Jeff Gutterman, who spent a multitude of hours seeking out information and writing what he learned. I pray that as you read and enjoy, you will see clearly that Gentile believers can be greatly used of God to bring salvation to God's Chosen People. That has been my delight for many years.

Ruth Wardell
Plano, Texas

As my wife Ana and I attended a Messianic Congregation in Dallas, Texas, we met and got to know Ruth Wardell, who had led Arnold Fruchtenbaum to the Lord. Ana had enrolled in an orientation class the congregation offered to familiarize people with Jewish faith, culture, and language. The teacher of this course was none other than Ruth. I often sat in the class with Ana.

We usually arrived early and, as a result, had many one-on-one conversations with Miss Ruth. These conversations blossomed into a history of Messianic missions. Each week, we heard about various works of the ministry—as well as the trials, tribulations, joys, and salvations Ruth had witnessed over the years.

Part of the course required that Ana read biographies of individuals who had ministered to Jewish people, as well as narratives about Jewish believers. She was deeply touched by these life stories and how Jewish people came to faith in Yeshua (Jesus' Hebrew name). She realized that Ruth had actually worked with some of these people and had accomplished much in Jewish mission work.

Listening to Ruth week after week, I became aware that she was validating my philosophy that Jewish and Gentile believers can be an effective team working together to witness to Jewish people. When I told this to Ana, she said, "Someone needs to write Ruth's story. Jeff, would you consider doing that?" I agreed. We approached Ruth with this idea, and at first, she was hesitant. But after some discussion, she agreed to work with me to chronicle her long and fruitful career in Jewish ministries.

The following work is the result of many fascinating hours of recording Ruth's memories and of interviewing the many people whose lives were so positively affected by this faithful Christian woman. I hope that after reading Ruth's story, you will be inspired and motivated to introduce Jewish people to their Messiah, Yeshua.

Jeffrey Gutterman
Melissa, Texas

TABLE OF CONTENTS

PREFACE ix

PROLOGUE xiii

CHAPTER 1 On My Way to New York City...1

CHAPTER 2 My Family 3

CHAPTER 3 The London Bible Institute..15

CHAPTER 4 The New York Years (1946 – 1973) 23

CHAPTER 5 My Beginnings at the American Board of Missions to the Jews

           (ABMJ) in 1946...29

CHAPTER 6 Mission Work 41

CHAPTER 7 Leaving Coney Island...51

CHAPTER 8 New Missions: Queens, Far Rockaway, Huntington Station,

           Lindenhurst, and Levittown, NY...65

CHAPTER 9 Summer Camp 81

CHAPTER 10 The Youth..91

CHAPTER 11 Balancing Your Life 115

CHAPTER 12 The California Years (1973 – 1993).......................................121

CHAPTER 13 Ministry for Senior Men and Women......................................127

CHAPTER 14 Classes for Younger Women...143

CHAPTER 15 Workers..149

CHAPTER 16 Texas (1993 – Present) 163

CHAPTER 17 Ruth's Musings/Reflections 169

POETRY 191

PROLOGUE

—When I was young, the only thing that I wanted to do was the will of God. I said, "When I get old, I want to be able to look back and say I've done the will of God." I was passionate about that, almost obsessed with it to a certain extent. Now I can look back and truly say, with all of my heart and with all of my soul, that my entire life, I strove to do the will of God. I'm still working on it, and I think that is the most important thing.

—The day that I was born was really the day that I began my ministry to the Jewish people. My father, a Baptist minister, chose the name Ruth for his daughter. In the Bible, Ruth said to Naomi, her Jewish mother-in-law, "Your people shall be my people, and your God, my God." My father never imagined how prophetic my name would become.

Ruth Wardell, 2011

CHAPTER 1
On My Way to New York City

I finally had received my assignment. After months of prayer, God had shown me where I was to do His work. I was on my way to the Big Apple, New York City, to fill a position with the American Board of Missions to the Jews (ABMJ). I was so excited and joyful that I thought I would burst at the seams. It felt as though I were walking on air. My earthly belongings were packed into two suitcases, and I was en route to begin a career in the mission field.

I settled into my seat on the train, which was taking me from my hometown of London, Ontario, to New York City. This was an overnight trip, and I would have much time on the train to meditate on my new job and all it would require. I did not have any knowledge or experience of the mission upon which I was about to endeavor.

At the tender age of twenty-two, I had no idea, nor could I have ever imagined, what awaited me at my new assignment with ABMJ. It finally dawned on me that I was answering the call of God on my life. I was going to be a missionary to the Jewish people in New York City.

Sitting in the sleeper car, I lifted the window blind and peered out onto the Hudson River. As the train sped along, it gently swayed back and forth, making its way on a southerly route along the eastern shore of the river to New York City. I recall that the trip was really quite pleasant. It was October 1, 1946. The leaves of the trees were just beginning to turn color for the fall season, and the view was breathtaking. As the train neared the city, the colorful forested scenery gave way to gray steel and towering cement structures. The train slowed noticeably as it glided into New York's Grand Central Station. I immediately searched for the directions I had written down regarding the location of the room that I was possibly going to rent.

I made my way to an apartment building in the Borough Park section of Brooklyn. I had just visited New York City the month before, when I was interviewed by Dr. Joseph Cohn, the son of Leopold Cohn (the founder of ABMJ). The mission had made arrangements for me to share a small apartment with someone who was looking for a roommate. Her name was Ceci, and after meeting her, it seemed as though she would make a nice roommate. I decided that I would stay there, and I rented the room on a weekly basis for five dollars. The building was ideally located. It was near a subway station with many connecting subway lines. That made my travels as a missionary much easier and very convenient.

The room that I rented had two beds, a little bathroom and a small area where I stored my two suitcases. Those suitcases contained everything that I owned. There was so much for me to learn, especially on how to travel around this immense city. I soon obtained a map to help me navigate through the streets and the subway system of New York City and its five boroughs. Every day was an adventure.

My First Day of Work—October, 1946

My first day of work had arrived. I traveled to ABMJ's mission in Coney Island and reported to a woman named Hilda Koser. She was referred to as "Miss Koser" by everyone at the mission. I was going to start working with the younger children. I had worked with children in Canada, so I confidently entered the room where fourteen preschool children were gathering and waiting for their new teacher. We quickly got to know each other, and the children and I had a fabulous day together. To this day, I still remember having one child on each knee and playing the piano while singing songs. It wasn't until some years later that I learned that Hilda Koser was unsure about my abilities. She had prayed, "Lord, I'll know that Ruth should stay on as a missionary, if none of the children cries today."

CHAPTER 2
My Family

Wardell Family—Harold, Maude, Ruth, Glenn, and Don

My father, Glen Wardell, was a Baptist minister, and my mother, Maude Wardell, had been trained as a nurse. My father was first and foremost an evangelist, and nothing pleased him more than to share the Word of God with all people. My father knew of the work of Hudson Taylor (b. 1832 – d.1905), a great English missionary to China who had founded the China Inland Mission. My mother and father had trained to go to China with the China Inland Mission as missionaries, and they were awaiting their assignment. Mother was very excited about the upcoming move to China. She was fascinated by the little shoes that the Chinese women would wear. They would bind their feet in order to fit into the shoes. My mother had even obtained a pair of these shoes for herself. They were almost ready to leave for China when they received disappointing news. My father had not passed the physical tests. This disqualified them from going to China as missionaries.

Disappointed but not dissuaded, my father began a career in ministry with a particular interest in missions. Wherever he ministered, he successfully searched out places where a Sunday School or a mission could be started to do the work of the Lord. In addition to having altar calls for people to receive Jesus as their Lord, my father would also call people forward to become missionaries. There always were people who responded to his call. Every few years, my family would move to a new location, which permitted my father to develop new ministries.

When the family lived in Oshawa, Ontario, my father would hold large missionary conferences, and he always highlighted the Chinese mission work because this was his first love. He could not be a missionary to China, but he had learned a great deal about the Chinese culture and encouraged people to go there as missionaries. This was in 1935, and sadly, just a few years later, the Chinese mission field was closed. After World War II, communists took over mainland China and did not allow any Christian missionaries to enter the country. That brought an end to mission work in China, but up until that time, missionaries had done a tremendous work there. Hundreds of missionaries had worked hard for many years, and they had opened huge schools where they taught the Chinese people about the Gospel. As a result of their work, untold numbers of Chinese people became believers in Jesus, and today there are approximately 50 million Chinese believers. Even though this is a small percentage of the current Chinese population, it is still a large number of people.

Glenn Wardell—Ruth's Father

Father believed a great deal in the power of prayer. He had a list of 1,000 missionaries for whom he consistently offered prayer, along with praying for his congregants. It was not unusual for him to have six or seven prayer meetings each week. There were prayer meetings before church on Sunday mornings and before the evening service Sunday evenings. On Sunday afternoons, Father would take people to work at the five or six Sunday Schools that he had planted, and he would hold a service in each one. Some of the people in these Sunday Schools got together and started churches.

In fact, not too many years ago, on a visit back to my hometown of Scarborough, Ontario, I was having lunch in a restaurant in the old neighborhood with my cousin. I said to her, "I wish that I had the time to go see the church that my father established many years ago in Kitchener Park, Ontario." I remember going there for the Christmas programs when I was a little girl. This particular church had started as just a small Bible study group in someone's house. It soon grew into a flourishing church and was still in existence at the time of my visit. A woman sitting next to us turned to me and said, "I just could not help overhearing your conversation. I'm a member of that church." I was pleasantly surprised that someone in a small, out-of-the-way restaurant was a member of a church that my father had planted some sixty years earlier. It was encouraging to hear her tell of all the blessings that God had bestowed down through the years.

My mother did not work full-time. However, she did go to people's houses to help them with their medical problems. She was a wonderful pastor's wife. She had attended Toronto Bible College at night to earn her degree. Once she married my father, she devoted her life to being the dutiful wife of Pastor Glen Wardell. My father depended on my mother, and she never let him down. I remember that my mother was often referred to as the best pastor's wife in Ontario. If someone in the church needed assistance, she would do all that she could to help. Everyone knew Maude Wardell. She was a great communicator and had an uncanny talent for speaking on her feet. Mother was a gifted teacher who taught the young women's classes with great creativity. She sang in the choir, was a "mother" to everyone, and was deeply loved. No one ever had an unkind word to say about her. In the same way that I had inherited my father's passion for missionary work, I also inherited my mother's creativity, which served me well in future years.

I was the youngest of three siblings. Both of my brothers, Donald and Harold, had been born on the Six Nations Indian Reservation where my father began a pastorate in 1919. Don was born in 1920, and Harold was born in 1922. When my father was disqualified from going to the mission field in China, he went to the Indian Tribes in Ontario. My father experienced much success there.

Wingham (1923 – 1926)

In 1923, my family moved to the small town of Wingham in southern Ontario. Wingham is about twenty-five miles east of the shores of Lake Huron. I visited Wingham in 2001, and I even visited the house where I was born and spent my first three years.

Ruth's First House

The town hasn't changed much, and the population has stayed around 3,000, as it was back when I came into the world on December 29, 1923.

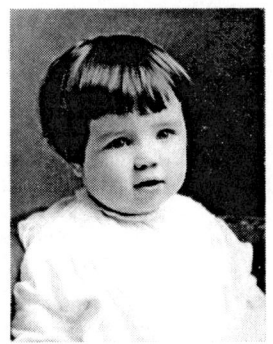

Ruth: 1924, 1year old

My dad named me *Ruth*. In the Bible, a person's Hebrew name indicated his or her personality or calling. My parents followed this tradition. For over sixty years, the Scripture verse taken from Ruth 1:16b has reflected my life, "Your people shall be my people and your God, my God."

Scarborough, Ontario (1926 – 1933)

In 1926, we moved to the town of Scarborough, just east of Toronto. The house that we lived in was at the bottom of a hill. It was a four-bedroom house. One of these bedrooms was used as a study for my father. I often slept there whenever we had visitors that stayed over because the visitors generally slept in my room. I have fond memories of my bedroom. There was a dresser that was fairly close to the bed. I was able to jump from the dresser to the bed, which I did quite often. This room also had an alcove in it where I used to quietly read by the light of the moon.

Being the youngest and the only girl in the family, I soon learned to play hard and even developed a mischievous streak. I can recall that my mother and father did not seem to know where I was most of the time. At least I don't think they knew. They would have had gray hair a lot sooner if they had any idea what I was doing. I was a typical tomboy. My brothers loved to have fun, and they delighted in teaching me the tricks of the trade. I took to these lessons and had a great time with my older brothers. Sometimes, we would slide down the Scarborough Cliffs on pieces of cardboard. When we reached the bottom, we would go swimming in the lake. I loved mischief as much as my brothers did. Once, we took wet clay and spread it all over our bodies, including our face and hair. We let the clay dry and harden. People would stare as they saw these three clay creatures walking along the beach.

Other times, we would run along little ledges on the side of the cliffs. I still shudder as I recall the path on the Scarborough Cliffs. These were high cliffs that went all the way down to Lake Ontario. There was a dirt path about halfway up that was just about wide enough for one's foot. One misstep meant a fall of 100 feet into the lake below. Oftentimes, when I would run along this path, dirt would slip from under my shoes, but I didn't have time to be afraid. I was having too much fun. Fear was never an issue. It never occurred to me that I could fall. Reflecting back on my early years, I have enjoyed the protection of Psalm 17:5, "My steps have held fast to Your paths. My feet have not slipped." This psalm has also sustained me through many other events in my life.

Once, I was hanging upside down by my ankles from a high tree branch. Suddenly, I found myself falling head first. A rough landing and certain serious injury was averted by my brother, Don, who caught me and in one motion turned me right-side up so that I landed on my feet. I know that every time that I have fallen short in my life, God in His mercy has faithfully undergirded me.

It was quite a long walk to get to school. There weren't any buses along that path. In the cold Canadian winter, my nose always seemed to freeze. As children, we really enjoyed our playtime even though the family did not have much money to buy toys and games. We lived near a large trash dump. My brother Don would often go rummaging through the piles of trash and find many items he could use to make playthings. He would help the neighborhood children make a lot of their toys. Once, we made stilts and had fun walking up and down the streets. We also made a lot of things out of old tires, which also came from the "dump."

Once, Don brought home an old clock and fixed it immediately. He could fix anything that he found that was broken. He would take a wooden spool that no longer had any thread and put two nails in the top. Then he would take a piece of tin and cut out a propeller, and then put the propeller on the spool over the two nails. Next, he would put the spool on a stick and wrap some string around and pull hard. The propeller would spin off the spool and go sailing into the air.

Sundays were joyous days for our family. All our activities centered on our love for Jesus. I was ten years old when I made a formal declaration of faith and gave my heart to the Lord. There comes a time in a person's life when one realizes that he or she is a sinner. I was quite fortunate that this realization came early in my life. The event leading up to this happened when my mother asked me if I had washed my hands before supper. I was not prone to telling lies, but this time I did. Almost immediately, I knew that I had sinned and, thus, was a sinner. This event is what God used to make me aware of my sinful nature. I knew that I was in great need of salvation.

I attended the children's meetings at the church, which were held on Friday evenings. Oftentimes, there were as many as 150 children in attendance. On occasion, evangelists would come and visit. One night, I went forward to the altar, confessed my sins, and made a profession of faith. The lesson I learned that day has stayed with me all my life. If people do not realize that they are sinners, then they will never have salvation. When I share about Jesus, the first thing people need to know is that they are sinners and that Jesus is the one who has paid the price for our sins. All they need to do is accept the free gift of salvation that Jesus provides. Shortly thereafter, I was baptized by my father. What a glorious day that was!

Looking back, my missionary endeavors first began when I was ten years of age. I would rise early on Sunday mornings, and before the church services would begin, I would go out with people from the church to hand out Bible tracts. Up and down the streets of Scarborough I would go, leaving tracts on the doors. In addition, I often accompanied my father on Sunday afternoons and helped him with his pastoral duties.

Leslie Street—Oshawa, Ontario (1933 – 1940)

In 1933, we moved again, this time to Oshawa, a city about thirty miles east of Toronto. It is best known for being a General Motors town. The house we lived in was located at 316 Leslie Street. I lived there until I turned thirteen.

During this time, my maternal grandfather, who was not a believer, came to live with us for a few years from 1935 to 1939. He was confined to his room because he suffered from dropsy, an ailment caused by his drinking problems. Dropsy is an old name for edema, the accumulation of excess water, often in the abdomen. Grandfather did teach me how to play chess and how to hammer a nail. He had some heart problems, but he still continued to smoke a pipe, contrary to the doctor's orders. As a result of being afflicted by dropsy, there were many times that the doctor would come to the house and drain fluid from his abdomen. In those days, doctors still made house calls. Grandfather was an avid reader, which made him a knowledgeable person, but amazingly, he never learned to write. I spent many days in the public library borrowing books for him to read.

Many people attempted to tell my grandfather about God's redemptive work, but I never heard him make a profession of faith. Grandfather eventually went to stay with one of my aunts who lived near Toronto. He passed away on the day of my graduation from Bible College. I remember waking up early that morning with a strong desire to pray for him. I know in my heart that, as a family, we provided him with much love and plenty of opportunities to become a believer.

Leslie Street House

The Leslie Street house consisted of three levels. My two brothers shared a bedroom on the third floor where father had his office. There were three bedrooms on the second floor, which were occupied by my parents, my grandfather, and me. My bedroom was directly below my brothers'. Don had obtained one of those crystal radio sets, which he assembled. There weren't any speakers on the crystal sets. You could only listen to the radio broadcasts by using an earphone. This was our generation's primitive version of today's "Walkman" or "iPod." My brothers listened to this radio with earphones in their room. Once in a while, they would drop a second set of earphones out the window, and I would bring it into my room so that I could listen to the radio. When my friends would sleep over, we would listen to that radio with such excitement. While the radio is quite commonplace in this age of high definition TVs and computers, back in the 1930s, it was quite unique and exciting to have a radio. Even so, books were our main source of entertainment.

My father spent much of his energy leading people to the Lord and planting churches, which meant that he was rarely at home. I was affected by the missionary spirit in my home from a young age and had the desire to be one. In church, one Sunday night when I was twelve years old, I answered the call to be a missionary and went forward. From that time on, my goal in life was to be a missionary. I knew that I wasn't the best preacher's kid that ever lived, but I always had a love for Jesus in my heart and a desire to serve Him. I used to dream of going to

Africa, and I imagined myself going in and out of the little grass huts there, sharing the Gospel.

It is interesting to note that in this small area of Ontario, near Toronto, many of my contemporaries had also received the call to the mission field. Classmates and neighbors were going off to Africa, China, India, South America, the West Indies, and other places around the world to share the Gospel message. In fact, it was unusual if one did *not* become a missionary.

Mary Street Public School

I attended the Mary Street Public School in Oshawa. The school was located near my house. Oftentimes, I would roller skate to school from Leslie Street, down a very long hill. These were street skates that would hook onto my shoes. I would tighten the front clamp with a skate key so the skates would fit snugly. As I sped down the hill toward the entrance to the school, at the very last moment, without missing a step, I would slip off my skates and run into the classroom. Roller skating to school afforded me some extra time to get ready in the mornings.

Mary Street School

I don't remember many of my teachers nor what I was taught. But I do vividly remember a game that the girls used to play at recess. Two rows of girls would line up facing each other, holding hands with the girl that we faced. Another girl would leap and throw her body across our arms. Then, we would throw the girl up in the air and forward until she had come to the end of the line. We would repeat this procedure until each girl had a turn. This activity was forbidden by the teachers because it held great risk of injury.

Simcoe Street House

Simcoe Street—Oshawa
(1936 – 1940)

After two years, the family moved yet again, to 191 Simcoe Street in Oshawa. This house was similar to the house on Leslie Street. In this house, I had the front bedroom, which also served as the guest room. Again, I quite often slept in my father's office due to the many guests that we would host. We had rabbits and chickens for pets, which we kept outside in our double garage. The chickens arrived as a result of a science experiment that I did for high school. The students had to bring in one dozen eggs and place them in an incubator. This produced one white chick and one black chick. I placed these chicks in a box and took them home with me on a streetcar. I was amused by the reactions of my fellow passengers to the loud chirping sounds. My grandfather helped me build a small pen for these chicks. Our chicken population increased when my father brought home four more chicks. It was fun to watch them grow up, and we always had plenty of eggs to eat, from then on.

Occasionally, a couple who lived in a house owned by my paternal grandparents in Toronto would come to visit. During their visits, we would bring the rooster into the house to feed it in the living room. I never knew how fearful this lady was about roosters until many years later. I had great fun bringing the rooster into the house. However, I never would have brought it into the house, had I known how petrified this dear woman was of it.

I have many splendid memories of Simcoe Street. Every Sunday, we had guests for dinner. On Sunday morning, Mother and I would set the table with an elegant tablecloth, cloth napkins, and silverware. Mother was a perfectionist, and table setting was no exception. She also demanded that we display proper manners. I am extremely thankful that I was taught these excellent qualities.

The Oshawa Collegiate and Vocational Institute (OCVI)

Oshawa Collegiate and Vocational Institute

There weren't any graduation exercises at our public school. Students just moved on to the next level. The next school I attended was my high school named The Oshawa Collegiate and Vocational Institute (OCVI). In grammar school, I had skipped the second grade which meant that I was younger than my classmates. I recall that the corridors of the school were long with high ceilings. At the time, it was the only high school in the town, and it served almost 1,000 students. High school in Canada lasted for five years. However, only a handful of students attended the fifth and final year. These students were the only ones eligible to go on to college. The rest of the students took courses such as automobile repair, woodworking, and vocational skills. My father insisted that my brothers and I attend the full five-year course so that we would be prepared for college. The courses in the five-year track were very demanding. I was required to take six major subjects consisting of English, French, Latin, History, Math, and Science. The elective courses included Typing, Cooking, Accounting, Sewing, etc. These courses were offered at 8 a.m., and I found them very helpful.

The Simcoe Street house was a little over one mile from the high school. Whereas the Mary Street Public School was downhill from my house, this time the path to school was uphill. Lunch was our main meal of the day. Mother made it mandatory that everyone had to come home for lunch. This meant that, going back and forth to school, we walked over four miles each day. While this trip did build my stamina, it also was somewhat draining.

One morning, Don and I were delayed, and we knew that we were going to be late for school. This was not something that we wanted to deal with since the school would make sure that our parents would be notified. We did not want to have to explain to our parents why we were late. My brother Don always had great ideas especially when facing a challenge. Right then and there, he developed a plan that would allow us to get to school on time. He grabbed the family bike and rode it for two blocks. I ran behind him. Don parked the bike by a lamp post and began running for the next two blocks. When I arrived at the bike moments later, I would hop on and pedal for another two blocks. I would pass my brother and arrive at the next meeting point, just before he came running up to change places with me. We repeated this procedure, until we arrived at school, thankfully, just before the late bell.

Just as with my elementary school years, I don't have any significant memories of my high school years except for Miss Armstrong, my French teacher. She does stand out in my memory because she threatened to cut off our noses and replace them with carrots if we didn't do our classwork. I was certainly motivated to learn French that year. When I visited France many years later, I was thankful for that motivation because I was able to converse in the French language.

A typical day in my high school years consisted of walking four miles back and forth to school, along with many church activities and challenging schoolwork. I had to repeat some of my third year courses because this demanding schedule caused fatigue, and my grades declined noticeably. After much renewed diligence and study, I successfully passed my courses. Shortly thereafter, in 1940, we moved again. This time it was to Islington, on the west side of Toronto.

Islington: The Years at the End of High School Leading to Bible School

We had moved from Oshawa to Islington in the year before my final year of high school. As a result, I was a little behind the rest of my class when I arrived in my new school. This was during World War II. The school administration decided to allow students in their last year of school to choose between writing their final exams and working for farmers at the market gardens. Working at the market gardens helped the war effort. Final exams in those days were not graded by a teacher in your school. The exams were sent down to a central grading center where the final exam paper was graded by a teacher from another school who did not know you. In August, the grades were printed in the newspaper.

I opted to go out to work in the market gardens, and I received whatever grade I had earned as a result of the work I had done in class up to that time. This suited me because I was behind in Latin as a result of having moved from one school to another in the middle of my fourth year. The Latin class in Oshawa was somewhat behind my new class in Islington, and I had a difficult time trying to catch up.

I worked in the market gardens for eight hours each day. We would grow carrots, tomatoes, and various other vegetables. I often worked my eight-hour day sowing carrots. I would walk up and down with a seed spreader. The gardens were not too far from my house, so I was able to ride my bicycle the two-to-three miles to work. I earned twenty-five cents per hour for a grand total of two dollars each day. The program that exempted me from school required that I work at the market gardens for eight weeks. I made ten dollars per week, and my mother took half my salary. The concept that many families had in those days was that if children were working, they should contribute half of what they earn to the family to help with food and other expenses. That left me five dollars per week to save for going to college. I saved my money. By the end of the summer, I had about twenty dollars. I graduated at the age of eighteen.

Mom Taylor

My mother was a good mother who cared deeply for her children, but she wasn't available to us as much as we would have liked because she also had the demands of being a pastor's wife. I was fortunate enough to have people in my life that helped fill that maternal void. One such person was Mrs. Taylor. I affectionately refer to her as "Mom T." Mrs. Taylor was a great influence

Mom Taylor and Ruth, 1946

in my younger life. Mom T. was a member of Dad's church and worked with the children's ministry as well as running the Vacation Bible School.

She did not have any children of her own but related well to young people and knew how to reach out to them. She held a prayer meeting before church on Sunday evenings at 6:30 p.m. for the young girls. I had to walk almost a mile to attend these prayer meetings, and I rarely missed one. This meeting took place in a small room with chairs all around its perimeter. During the meeting, each of these chairs had a little girl kneeling on the floor in front of the chair, praying fervently to the Lord.

Mom Taylor seemed to really understand some of the things that I would occasionally do. Some of those things weren't so good. I was a mischievous young lady. One time, while I was walking down the street with Mom T., I ran ahead and knocked on the door of a house. I would quickly run back to Mom T.'s side. By the time the person who lived there came to answer the door, we were already past the house. The person who opened the door would be looking for the one who had knocked. He or she never suspected that this sophisticated-looking woman and this young girl, slowly walking along the street, were the pranksters who had disturbed him or her. The person at the door could only see our backs since we were already well past the house. If they could see our faces, they would have seen us chuckling quietly, repressing the desire to burst out laughing.

I have worked mostly with children throughout my life, and I'm still dedicated to educating children in the things of the Lord. I love children, and to this very day, I have the ability to understand and to fit in with a child's desire to have fun in very much the same way that Mom T. did with me. I learned much from Mrs. Taylor. She also encouraged me to learn how to play the piano. I found that music was essential when working with young people, as well as with adults. She greatly influenced me and truly was a gift from God. We were close friends until her death. She went home to be with the Lord during the time I was in Long Island in the late 1960s. This was a great loss for me.

My father and brothers also had the same mischievous side to their personalities. Whenever I would engage in mischievous behavior, my father rarely corrected me. Sunday was always a day when we would have guests at our house. One time, my brothers wired the wicker cane chairs in the dining room, where our guests, who were friends of the family, would be sitting. Of course, these wires were not visible since they were intertwined within the wicker. They would hook up the wires to a hand-held DC generator, which I would hold. My father used to sit there knowing exactly what I was getting ready to do. I would look over at him, and he would just sit there and grin. I sat there quietly and politely with my father and his friends. When no one was looking, I would reach under my chair and slowly turn up the power. Of course, the unsuspecting guests didn't have a clue as to what was happening. I would watch the people begin to squirm on the seats. These people did not want to seem undignified, and they would try to hide their discomfort. It was at this point that I would quickly turn the power down. After a few minutes, I would turn the power up just a bit higher. By faith, I had received eternal salvation, but I was not sanctified in this area. While my dad went along with these pranks, I can only remember one time he was agitated with me, because I did not obey my mother, which was strictly forbidden.

Growing up in and around the city of Toronto and smaller towns in Ontario, Canada, was not that much different than growing up in the United States. Of course, there was much more snow, and it was colder. Toronto was a very big city, and we always seemed to live on the edge of town. It was good growing up there. The people were kind, and the schools were good.

Even though my brothers and I lacked material things and had to share our family time with the church congregants, our home was spiritually rich. My early years were filled with days of hard playing, singing, and church attendance. I would spend many hours reading the Word of God and memorizing Scripture passages. This practice has served me well over the years, and it is one in which I still engage, even to this present day.

After my high school graduation, I attended London Bible Institute in Ontario, starting in the fall of 1942. The London Bible Institute no longer exists. It joined with Toronto Bible College and today has become Tyndale University College and Seminary.

CHAPTER 3
The London Bible Institute

The London Bible Institute was located about two-and-a-half hours from my home. Tuition was ten dollars per semester. Looking back after all these years, it seems a little silly for a school to charge so little, but this was a school established on faith that God would supply its needs. It was a blessing to see how God supplied the needs of the school week by week. I especially remember one extremely cold winter day. We had a long prayer meeting with our coats on. We prayed for enough money to pay the heating bill, or classes would have to be cancelled. Somehow the Lord answered our prayer, and we were back to classes the next day. Watching how God blessed the school certainly gave all of the students a good example of how God can and does supply needs.

London Bible Institute

The school building was an old, large house. Classes were held on the bottom floor. Most of the time, we all sat together in the same room. When I started my studies, there were twelve students in my class. There had been fewer students in the years before my class. The following year there were thirty students, and the year after, fifty or sixty. London Bible Institute grew and added new teachers to accommodate the increasing student population. They also moved across the street to a bigger house after I left in 1945.

I had saved twenty dollars from my work at the market gardens. I paid ten dollars for tuition which meant that I had ten dollars left for the semester. Out of necessity, I had to get some work rather quickly to be able to continue my education. I looked around and found a job in a soap factory. I once again earned twenty-five cents per hour. I worked at the factory Monday through Friday after class, from 1 p.m. to 5 p.m. and Saturday morning from about 8 a.m. to 12 noon, earning six dollars per week. Room and board at the dormitory where I lived cost five dollars per week which left one dollar. I would give sixty cents to the Lord as an offering which left forty cents for the week. I didn't go anywhere or buy anything. I rode my bicycle anywhere I needed to go. Forty cents didn't get you very much at all, even in the 1940s.

Every once in a while, a church friend from years before, or someone else, would send a few dollars, which I always appreciated. Somehow, I got through. I didn't worry about money because most people didn't have very much. We were all working hard for our money. At the soap factory, there were mostly Christian workers. I rather enjoyed my times in the afternoons. Of course, there were no deductions on your earnings. If you earned six dollars, you received six dollars. The food at school was not always good, but thankfully the ladies at the soap factory brought sandwiches, cakes, and cookies for me to eat.

Ruth's Graduating Class, 1945

My dormitory was a big house with four bedrooms upstairs. Eight of us shared the upstairs in this home. It seemed that, in the dormitory, I was always getting into a little trouble. One day, I sat on my bed, and it broke. That got me into a bit of trouble. I wasn't at the school for too long when I awkwardly bumped into the two boards that were covering a stove pipe hole leading down into the living room below. Half of the board fell down into the living room and hit a man on his shoulder as he was passing by. My reputation in this school was going from bad to worse, but I didn't know that. I was just happy to be in school preparing for whatever God had for me.

The next year, I was in a bigger dormitory that housed about sixteen of us. They wanted to have a meeting to choose one girl to be head over the dormitory. The dean's wife explained the responsibilities of this position, and then she asked the girls to vote for one of the group to be given this job. There were only two of us there from the year before, and the new students had been asking us questions about everything and anything. I was the one they chose to head the dorm. The dean's wife was supposed to sit with the chosen person and explain what the rules would be. When she saw that I had been chosen, she just left without saying a word. I took the initiative and set up rules for when we would study, how we would do things in the dorm, etc. If someone got home five minutes late after the dorm was locked for the night, they could get into a lot of trouble with the school administration. Those who did come late would throw a pebble at my window, and I would come down and let them in. We had a great time in my dormitory.

The school's founder was an older man named Dr. Mahood. I don't suppose that he was paid a large salary since the school did not have a lot of money. Whenever he talked, his teeth would clack together. We all used to run to take seats in the back of the class so that we did not have to hear this constant clacking. I do remember that I learned the Book of Revelation in his class.

During my second year of school, I became very sick and was diagnosed with a leaky heart valve. One time, I went into sort of a coma for four hours, and nobody knew what was happening to me. I came out of all of that. The doctors were careful with me for a while. I managed to stay in school, attend class, and pass all of my tests. School came easy for me. It was a good time. It was three years of being away from home and trying to grow up—and all the things that go along with that.

There was a Jewish student at this school named Louis Wineke. He came from Germany where his father had been a great businessman. The story of how he came to be at London Bible Institute was quite interesting. There was a woman who dedicated her life to getting young people out of Germany so that they wouldn't be killed in the persecution of the Holocaust. She was a believer in Jesus. She was able to get Louis and many other Jewish young people out of Germany. During the trip to a safe place, she would share the Gospel of Jesus with them. Louis received Jesus as his Messiah and became a great believer as a result of this woman's sharing the Gospel. He was eventually sent to us in Canada. We were too young to understand what this young man from Germany was doing at this Bible School. We didn't know how to relate to him other than to try to make him feel comfortable and at home with us. We soon became good friends. We used to compare grades on exams to see who would get 100 on the tests. He was a very smart person, so he would win most of the time. I would get 99s, and he would get 100s.

For three years, Louis never heard a word from his parents or his sister. He did not know what had happened to them. I did pray for him when he went back to Germany after the war. Praise God, he found his entire family alive and well. They had been able to hide from the Nazis in Switzerland and other places. That was my introduction to becoming friendly with someone who was Jewish. We became good friends and talked a lot. The three-year course was not bad, and I did learn a lot of things. However, they didn't have any courses about teaching children. It was the hand of God that led me just where I needed to be.

My Call to the Mission Field

In 1945, when I was twenty-one years old, I graduated from The London Bible Institute. Most of my classmates went to the mission field immediately after graduation. I watched my classmates excitedly prepare to leave for their posts in mission fields around the world. My first roommate went to the Sudan, another went to a different place in Africa, and yet another went to Jamaica in the West Indies.

As I watched my friends venture out to various parts of the world, I did not have a clue as to where I would go. I was certain that God had a place for me. I longed only to follow His plan for my life, and I knew that since He is faithful, He would in His time, reveal the plan to me.

Some young people who had left for the mission field returned in one year or less. Some were disillusioned or overwhelmed by the missionary lifestyle. Many of them came back because of illness. Others were involved in disputes with their fellow workers. There were all kinds of reasons that a person did not last long on the mission field. I believe that if one is called to the mission field, God will undoubtedly make it clear where one should toil. I was determined not to rush, but to wait for clear direction from the Lord.

I prayed day after day for a clear sign. Days became weeks, weeks became months, and still all was silent. I worked in four Vacation Bible Schools that summer. I occupied the time. I had worked with children in my father's church since I was fifteen. While waiting for God to reveal His will for my life, I was busy helping in the Sunday School classes and the children's ministry at my father's church. At this point, I considered following in my mother's footsteps by studying to become a nurse, perhaps a missionary nurse. I obtained the necessary papers to apply for a nursing program in the U.S. To become a nurse, I needed to have my tonsils removed, and I had to fully recover before my application would be accepted. This I did. I completely filled out and submitted the required application.

It was then that I heard about a school in Dallas, Texas, called the Child Evangelism Institute. This organization had a six-month program that trained and prepared people to go into children's ministry. This appealed to me as I had developed a love for teaching children. The only thing that I needed was the $500 tuition to pay for this school. One day, while I was riding my bicycle, I said, "Lord, if you give me $500, I will know that you want me to go to this school." I expected that nobody would give $500 for what was probably considered no good reason—that is, unless God was in it. So, if God was going to be in it and provide the $500, I knew that I was to attend this training program.

Isabel Smith

Ruth and Isabel Smith, 1945

Isabel Smith was an older woman who was serving as a missionary to the Jewish people in Hamilton, Ontario. She exhibited a great love for God's Chosen People, the Jews. We both attended the London Bible Institute at the same time, but she was one year ahead of me. I knew her because the school was small in size, and everyone was fairly well-acquainted with each other.

Isabel called and asked me to come visit her in Hamilton, which is located on the western point of Lake Ontario, about seventy-five miles east of London. Isabel did not have much in the way of finances. She earned about $100 each month, which barely covered her expenses. However, she had succeeded in saving approximately $700. People in those days did not save large sums of money. They gave sacrificially. Isabel recounted to me that she knew God wanted me to have $500 from the money she had saved. She did not question God. Rather, she responded in obedience.

I excitedly went to pick up the $500. I was twenty-one years old and quite aware that God was answering my prayer. It was exciting and humbling at the same time. Isabel was known as a spiritual, godly person, so this gift meant something to me. I anticipated that something special was on its way. When we met, Isabel related how God had instructed her to give me the $500. She told me that she was working for an organization called the American Board of Missions to the Jews. I had never heard of this organization, and it never occurred to me that I should go to work with the Jewish people. In fact, it was the furthest thought from my mind.

Isabel had been praying that five people from the London Bible Institute would go into Jewish missions. Isabel had said to God, "I do not want to give this money to just anyone. I want to give it to Jewish missions." The Lord answered Isabel's petition, and she was encouraged. He told her not to worry because she would indeed be giving it to Jewish missions. The Lord revealed to Isabel that I was one of the five. He told her, "Just give the money to Ruth, and it will be all right." When I went to pick up the money, Isabel already knew in her spirit that I was going to be a missionary to the Jews. She did not share this fact with me at the time.

We had planned that I would stay overnight. While I was in Isabel's house getting ready for bed, I was reading the Bible. I read Matthew 10:5–6: "These twelve Jesus sent out after instructing them: 'Do not go in the way of the Gentiles, and do not enter any city of the Samaritans; but rather, go to the lost sheep of the house of Israel.'" The verse seemed to leap off the page. Immediately, I understood. In an instant, I knew what God had wanted me to do. He wanted me to be a missionary to the Jewish people. Unquestionably, this was God's call on my life. I ran into Isabel's room and said, "I think God is calling me to the Jewish people," and I showed her the Scripture I had just read. Isabel was really excited to see God answering her prayers right before her eyes. The fact that God had shared with Isabel ahead of time that I would be a missionary to the Jewish people confirmed the call.

It is amazing and wonderful to see how God shows us what He would have us do. I feel that Isabel was so sensitive and wise in not telling me about the call to Jewish missions. She remained silent and waited for God to reveal this to me. She was mature enough to know that if God really called a person, then He would call that person Himself and not use another to relay the message.

As a twenty-one year old, that call was more than anything that I could have ever thought up by myself. God provided the money, the call to Jewish missions, and the confirmation of that call. The Lord knew that I needed all of those signs. As I reflect, I am very grateful for the situation that brought about the call. When one goes into Jewish missions, it is not easy. As events during my time as a missionary took place, it helped me to remember God's beautiful calling. I believe that for a Gentile, it is a high privilege to be called to the Jewish people, God's Chosen People. When I realized the depth of the call that I had received, I thought, "God, you really do love me. You gave me this joy to be with the Jewish people." That was a very exciting night for me.

Growing up in Ontario, I did not have any exposure to Jewish people. My father had been on the Board of the Toronto Jewish Missions in the past, but I don't recall ever meeting a Jewish person, let alone having any knowledge of Judaism. Even so, I did pray for Jewish people. The only thing that mattered to me was doing the will of God. My only concern was staying in the will of God. I was ready to go anywhere and do anything God wanted me to do. I needed to be certain that this was indeed God's will. I had come to understand that being in the will of God is a great place because that is where you find peace and real joy when "doors" open and opportunities present themselves. God doesn't always reveal His will for you immediately, and in my case he kept me waiting for seven months after graduation. This waiting period kept me yielded to do His will.

Now that I had the necessary funds, I prepared to travel to Dallas in January of 1946. I was ready to attend the Child Evangelism Institute for my preparation to work with Jewish children. I already had all of the papers necessary to come to the U.S. as a student because of my previous application to study nursing. Since it was already near the end of December, I was thankful that I already had the papers, since time was running out to start school on the first of January. Once again, God provided everything that I needed at the right time.

God was gracious to me, and I had a fantastic time learning about working with children. If I had left the London Bible Institute and gone directly into mission work, I wouldn't have gone into the field where I was supposed to be. The Lord always knows where to take us and what to present to us.

Child Evangelism Institute

The classes at the Child Evangelism Institute in Dallas took place from January through June of 1946. During this time, I lived with a family from the local Dallas area. Classes were held in the morning from 8 a.m. until noon. In my estimation, this school provided me with excellent training, especially in the area of teaching children from various age groups. Lesson planning and ministering to young children were highly emphasized. This Child Evangelism

Institute was a gift from above. The training that I received proved very useful in the years that followed. In fact, the notes that I took in these classes helped me tremendously throughout my ministry. While I had worked with children in the past, I didn't have any formal training in the areas that were covered at the Child Evangelism Institute.

Ruth Studying in Dallas, 1946

Interestingly, during those six months, I didn't participate much with child evangelism. Outside of my class time, I was studying for very difficult exams. The faculty members were well-qualified and had exercised good communication skills with the students.

I had never shared the story of Isabel Smith with my parents until I arrived in Dallas. All they knew was that I was going to Texas for training in child evangelism. I decided to write a letter to my parents and inform them that I had received my "call from God" and that this call was to go to the Jewish people. I believed that what I would share in this letter would be somewhat of a disappointment to my father. My parents had not been permitted to go to a foreign mission field due to health reasons. They had hoped that one day I would go to China or some other foreign country as a missionary, thus fulfilling the dream that was never fulfilled in their lives. However, Father did witness firsthand how I had waited patiently on the Lord for Divine direction. Once I received this direction, I was decisive. They were aware that the necessary finances had been provided for me and that I desired to follow God's plan. My mother was glad that I had discerned God's will for my life.

Sadly, I meet very few people who are really doing God's will. I strongly contend that if you really want to do the will of God, then He will open all the necessary doors in such marvelous ways. I was twenty-one when all of this transpired, and as I look back over more than sixty years, I have discovered that the act of placing God first in my life was a quieting force that saw me through many of the rough avenues that I encountered.

CHAPTER 4
The New York Years
(1946 – 1973)

The Next Stage: ABMJ New York

In July of 1946, after finishing my six-month course of study in Texas, I returned to Canada and worked at a camp for the summer. It was during this summer that I heard there was a position available in New York City as a Children's Leader with the American Board of Missions to the Jews (ABMJ). Today, ABMJ is known as Chosen People Ministries (CPM). I decided to contact them. This mission had been founded in the 1890s by an Orthodox rabbi, Leopold Cohn, who had come to faith in *Yeshua*/Jesus as his Messiah. The mission had accomplished great things in its fifty-plus years of existence. One of the reasons, among many others, I chose this mission was that this was the very same organization that Isabel Smith worked for in Hamilton, Ontario, and I knew that they had a good children's program.

Sadly, as sometimes happens in ministries, ABMJ had just experienced a split in their leadership. When the President of the London Bible Institute found out that I was thinking of going to work for them, he advised me not to go. He was sympathetic to the group that had split off from the mission. I felt that God wanted me to go to ABMJ, regardless of what had happened. I decided to work there for six months and thought that, if things didn't work out, I could explore other options. I was directed by the Lord to go to ABMJ, and that's where I went.

Summer's End Prophecy Conference
August 1946

During this same time, I was planning to go to New York for a meeting hosted by ABMJ called the Summer's End Prophecy Conference. It was held every year at the end of August.

The ABMJ administrators told me that I should attend this conference so they could meet with me and evaluate me for the teaching position.

I attended the conference that summer and interviewed with Dr. Joseph Hoffman Cohn, the son of Leopold Cohn, founder of ABMJ. The interview lasted ten minutes, and I was conditionally hired. It was agreed that I would come to New York on October 1 and work for three months. If they were satisfied with my work, and I was enjoying what I was doing, I would be hired permanently.

Don Wardell
Canadian Army

I stayed for the conference and rented a room for the week in Manhattan on 57th Street. ABMJ's home office was on 72nd Street. After paying for my round trip train fare and room, I didn't have any more money. My oldest brother Don had heard that I had gone to New York, so he came to meet me. We had always visited places together, and he was always happy to be with his sister. He thumbed his way down to New York since he didn't have any money, either. Along the way, he stopped at a beekeeper's place and did some work for him. Don earned ten dollars, and he brought this money with him to New York. The ten dollars fed us for one entire week. We ate most of our meals in Riverside Park, near the mission on 72nd Street.

Don had been stationed in England and Scotland throughout his Army career. He had just gotten out of the Canadian Army, having served during World War II, and he was living with my parents in Canada. After his discharge from the Army, he hitchhiked his way all across America. When he wasn't hitching rides in cars, he would take a flight on an airline. Since he still wore his uniform, he was allowed to fly for free, just after the war.

Isabel Smith was also in town for the conference. All mission employees attended the Summer's End Conference. When Isabel extended a dinner invitation to Don and me, I responded immediately and said, "Why don't you have dinner with us this evening? We are going to have dinner in the park." Isabel responded, "Oh, that would be nice," and she gave me one dollar. I came back to Don and told him that we now had one extra dollar. I was able to buy some extra food for our dinner in the park that evening with our friend Isabel.

While we were in New York, Don and I visited many of the tourist sites. We rode the subways for fun. A trip to the famous Coney Island Amusement Park in Brooklyn was a five-cent ride, one way. We couldn't resist visiting the Empire State Building. The Big Apple was just another playground for us, albeit a new and exciting playground. While I had stayed in a rented room during this conference, Don stayed at a Christian boarding house. He volunteered to answer the phone and earned his keep. This was very typical for him to do.

Don would meet me at the mission on 72nd Street every day and attend the meetings which we thoroughly enjoyed.

After the conference, I returned home to Canada to pack my belongings to begin my first assignment as a missionary with ABMJ on October 1, 1946.

A Short Historical Timeline of Chosen People Ministries

[*Editor's note*: Thousands of Jewish people came to faith in their Messiah through the work of missionaries in many organizations. Ruth Wardell was called to the American Board of Missions to the Jews (now Chosen People Ministries) and labored for over forty years. She had the satisfaction of seeing many Jews find salvation in the person of the Jewish Messiah, Yeshua, Jesus. Chosen People Ministries has a long, interesting, and fruitful history. Below is a short historical timeline of this mission to give some background of the organization Ruth joined.]

Leopold Cohn

1894—Rabbi Leopold Cohn, an Orthodox rabbi from East Hungary, founded a ministry in the Brownsville section of Brooklyn, New York, a short time after accepting Jesus as his Messiah. This ministry was known as the Brownsville Mission to the Jews. Cohn's vision was to share the Good News of Yeshua, Jesus, with his Jewish brothers and sisters. To assist in the acculturation of the many new immigrants to America, the mission offered services and Bible studies in Yiddish (the international language of European Jews), as well as classes to help people learn English, sewing, and other skills that would help secure employment. While there was tremendous opposition from the Jewish community, there were also many Jews who heard and responded to the Gospel through the teachings of this mission.

1897—The mission grew and established its headquarters in Williamsburg, Brooklyn. It was renamed The Williamsburg Mission to the Jews.

1911—Leopold's son, Joseph Hoffman Cohn, joined in the work of the mission.

1924—The mission grew to international status and was once again renamed. It was now known as the American Board of Missions to the Jews (ABMJ).

1937—Leopold Cohn died on December 11. Joseph Hoffman Cohn succeeded his father as the leader of the mission. He greatly expanded the vision of the mission.

1953—Joseph Hoffman Cohn died on October 5.

1984—The name of the ministry changed once again to Chosen People Ministries (CPM), as it is known today. With worldwide mission stations, CPM has continued the work of Leopold Cohn to this day. Dr. Mitch Glaser is the current leader.

Dr. Joseph Hoffman Cohn

Joseph Hoffman Cohn

Dr. Joseph Hoffman Cohn was the son of Leopold Cohn, the founder of the Williamsburg Mission to the Jews, which became American Board of Missions to the Jews, which became Chosen People Ministries. Joseph Cohn was in charge of the mission when I showed up in 1946. He was a very astute man and could sum up people quite accurately when he met them.

Joseph Cohn was a marvelous teacher, and today, after more than sixty years, I still remember the things he taught. He taught one lesson about the Seven Feasts of the Lord found in Leviticus 23. He would line up seven chairs for the seven feasts, and then he would sit on a different chair as he told about each of the Feasts. He was well known in churches all over the United States, and he was much sought after as a speaker. He followed in his father's footsteps, and he loved his work and his ministry. While his father's ministry was local in its influence, under Joseph, the mission extended all over the U.S. and into many countries worldwide.

By the time I came to New York, ABMJ was a very large mission due to the work and influence of Joseph Cohn. In 1946, it was estimated that ABMJ was doing a majority of U.S. missionary work to Jewish people—and that the other missions did the remainder of the work. Whatever the actual percentages were, ABMJ was doing a great amount of work in the Jewish mission field. In 1938, Joseph helped the founders of the Friends of Israel Ministry to get started. Friends of Israel is a wonderful organization that ministers to the Jewish people and shares the Gospel with them. Joseph helped many other missions as well.

Whenever I would meet with Joseph Cohn, we would sit for a while and I would share with him the work that we were doing. Before I left, he would raise his hands and pronounce a blessing over me. When I came to New York in September of 1946 to have my interview with him, he said that he thought I would like to work there and that they would be happy to have me. Over the years, I didn't have that many opportunities to talk with him. I did admire his commitment to this mission. He began new ways of reaching out to the Jewish community. He went on the radio, which was the latest technology. He was a well-loved man. Even after he died in 1953, radio stations continued to broadcast his messages for some time. I think that he was a marvelous leader in this mission.

Dr. Daniel Fuchs

After the death of Joseph Cohn in 1953, there were four men being considered to head the mission: Dr. Emil Gruen, Mr. John Pretlove, Dr. Henry Heydt, and Dr. Daniel Fuchs. The Board of Directors decided to divide the work of the mission among these four men. Daniel Fuchs was put in charge of all the missionaries at that time. I got to know him somewhat as a result of his heading up our division. He was always very kind to me, and

Dr. Daniel Fuchs

he let me do what I wanted, when I wanted to do it. I was creative, and I created many things that were useful to the mission's work. He came to our Christmas program, and it seemed that if he saw that your Christmas program was going well, and you had a lot of children attending summer camp, then he never bothered you. If all was going well, he figured that you were doing a good job. Eventually, he was chosen to lead the mission.

Daniel Fuchs grew up in the mission. As a child, he was influenced by Miss Sussdorf, a woman who had been with ABMJ for a very long time. She was an instrumental part of his coming to know the Lord. Miss Sussdorf also witnessed to his mother. His sister Judy worked in the mission for quite some time, as well.

Miss Augusta Sussdorf

I worked in the New York metropolitan area for twenty-seven years, from 1946 through 1973. When I came to New York, I met a most remarkable woman by the name of Augusta Sussdorf. Miss Sussdorf had started with ABMJ in 1903 as a volunteer.

She was a Gentile who loved the Lord and the Jewish people. She worked in a millinery for six months out of the year and saved enough money so that she could work for the mission for the remaining six months. Eventually, she was hired full-time. She

Miss Augusta Sussdorf

became the first female missionary worker to be hired by ABMJ in 1912. She worked and helped greatly in the Brooklyn Mission with Helen Koser, the mother of Hilda Koser, as well as Daniel Fuchs. She was instrumental in all of their salvations.

Most of her missionary years took place in a time called the "Golden Age of Jewish Missions." The missions at that time were set up as community centers, and various classes were held during the week. At one point in her career, Miss Sussdorf worked with Jewish mothers and girls in sewing classes and in Saturday morning Bible classes. On Sunday afternoons, she was present for meetings at the mission. She also did home visitations, distribution of clothes to the needy, and served in the medical dispensary three times a week.

Almost all of these activities were still in existence when I arrived in 1946, and it was not long before my schedule resembled the work that Miss Sussdorf had done for those many years. She was a woman with a zeal for the souls of people. She ministered with a lot of love.

CHAPTER 5
My Beginnings at
the American
Board of Missions
to the Jews (ABMJ)
in 1946

ABMJ 72nd St.
Headquarters, 1947

When I arrived at ABMJ in 1946, it was quite different than when Leopold Cohn had established the mission in 1894. In 1946, all of the Jewish missions were in a slump. There was not as much immigration in 1946 as there had been around the turn of the century, and people were not coming to the mission in the large numbers they had in years past. Over 3.5 million Jewish people came to the U.S. in the late 1800s through the early part of the 1900s. When Jewish people first arrived in large numbers in the 1890s, few of them knew anyone in this new country. They also knew nothing about this new culture. By 1946, Jewish immigration was down to a fraction of what it was in the early years of the mission. This was a result of the Holocaust, which had claimed the lives of six million Jews in Europe. Understandably, Jewish people did not want to attend a Christian mission after the Holocaust because Hitler had killed their family members in the name of Christ.

On my first day of work at the Coney Island Mission, Hilda Koser watched and waited as I worked with fourteen young children. I vividly remember having one child on each knee while I played the piano and sang songs with the children. At the end of the class, not one child had cried or even whimpered. The only ones who expressed any unhappiness were the parents of the little ones. When they came to pick up their children, many said, "You mean my child didn't cry? So, how come my child didn't cry? She always cries when I leave her. She didn't miss me?" I somberly told them, "No, your child didn't miss you." Since not one child had cried, Hilda Koser recommended me for the job.

God makes the "unusual" into "usual" to work out His plans for our lives. I worked in Coney Island for eight years and enjoyed the many weekly classes of children whom I taught the Word of God.

I worked day after day, and no one said a word about my performance. I thought that they must have been satisfied with my work since they had kept me on. When one thinks about what is involved in working with a mission today, it seemed so much simpler then. Today, if one wants to work for a mission, there are tests to take, forms to fill out, and doctrinal statements that one must agree with. It was just so much easier back in 1946. The days turned into weeks, and weeks became months. After six months on the job, I still absolutely loved what I was doing. By that time, I was teaching classes every day, as well as helping out with the older folks in the Old Brooklyn Mission, which included working in the dispensary.

Manhattan, Coney Island, and the
Old Brooklyn Mission

I was assigned to work in Manhattan, Coney Island, and the Old Brooklyn Mission. The Brooklyn Mission was where Leopold Cohn had worked in the late 1800s and early 1900s. I had become a missionary to the Jewish people. I knew almost nothing about Jewish people and knew even less about Messianic Jewish believers, so I began to read stories about them. One of those I read about was Leopold Cohn, the founder of ABMJ.

These were God's Chosen People, and I was young and inexperienced and didn't know how to go about my work. Since there was nobody to teach me how to be an effective missionary to the Jewish people, I decided to start my own training program. I went home and took out some note paper. I began to write a list of those things that I felt I needed to learn to do my job well. Some of the things that I wrote on this list included playing the piano better, cultivating a knowledge of the Jewish holidays and Messianic prophecies,

Brooklyn Mission—Williamsburg Mission

visiting Jewish homes, and learning more about Messianic Jews. It was quite a list. There were many hours spent traveling from mission station to mission station by subway train, so I used this time to memorize many of the Messianic prophetic verses in the Old Testament. Often, I would be so engrossed in the Scriptures that I would miss my stop. As the weeks went by, I would check off those items on the list that I had mastered and would add new things to learn as they arose. This worked quite well. As time went on, I learned much of what I needed to know.

To learn about home visits, I went to fellow workers who had experience doing this work. I soaked in everything I could learn from these people, and it helped me greatly. I remember an older woman named Mrs. Frank who had experience making visits to Jewish homes. She was supposed to go out with me to teach me how to reach Jewish people effectively. I liked her. She was a wonderful Jewish believer, but she didn't have too much methodology in what she did, so I did not learn too much from her. If she went out with me three times, that was a lot. What I did learn from Mrs. Frank was what it meant to be Jewish. I learned a lot about Jewish people from this lovely lady. On Sunday afternoons, I would go to the services held by the mission. Back in that era, the mission met on Sunday afternoons because some of the people would attend their local churches on Sunday mornings. ABMJ required that all of the workers attend the afternoon services in Manhattan at the 72nd Street Mission. Occasionally, I would play the piano. I was not the greatest pianist, so I would start practicing early Sunday morning for the afternoon's musical pieces. I wish I knew then what I know now about playing the piano.

On Mondays, I would be at the Beth Sar Shalom station in Coney Island with the children's class for the entire afternoon session. These were all Messianic Jewish children whose mothers were attending the women's Bible classes.

On Tuesdays, I would generally work in the Old Brooklyn Mission where we did visitations in the morning and part of the afternoon. We would go to apartment buildings and knock on doors, hand out tracts and invite people to the mission. Some of the reactions that we received were polite, while others just silently closed the doors of their apartments. Others were not really rude or unfriendly, but as they closed their doors, they would say, "We don't want anything to do with that." Others would ask, "How can you possibly do this to us?" Behind their closed doors, they would quickly call others in the building to warn them that Christians were in the building trying to convert Jews.

Joseph Hoffman Cohn's Evangelism Experience

One lesson that we were taught was a particular strategy that Joseph Hoffman Cohn learned from his experiences and described in his book *I Have Fought a Good Fight* (New York, 1953), page 42.

He wrote, "Joseph Hoffman Cohn, boy evangelist, distributed proselytizing tracts in tenements, beginning on the first floor and working up. By the time he was back down, the speed-reading Jews pelted him from above with hot soup and bombarded him with pots, pans, and garbage. Thus, I learned that the next time I went into a tenement I must start on the top floor and work down."

Joseph Cohn did these visitations in the late 1890s. We were doing this just after World War II, and the concentration camps were still fresh in these people's minds. Many had lost friends and relatives in Europe, and some had even emigrated recently after spending years in the camps. It was a very difficult time. I found it hard to relate to the terrible stories that I heard about what had happened. These people were not thrilled about a missionary coming to tell them to believe in Jesus since they perceived Jesus as a Christian and Christians as enemies. They believed that Christians hated Jews. And why wouldn't they feel that way? Hitler had stated that his Final Solution of Jewish extermination was being done in the name of Christ. Missionaries were considered to be as much of a threat to Jewish existence as the Nazi Holocaust had been. Why should they believe in the same Jesus who wanted them dead? To say the least, the reception that missionaries received when they went into these apartment buildings was quite contentious. Starting on the top floor of an apartment building and working our way down meant that it would be a lot easier to run down the few remaining floors than to run a gauntlet from the top all the way down to the street. I guess my years of rushing to school to avoid being late paid off, since I was pretty quick in getting out of the building once the alarm had been sounded. I was never hit by any projectiles. Other workers from the mission were not so fortunate and did not get out fast enough, so they were pelted mercilessly.

In all of my visitations over the period of a couple of years, I did not find many people who would speak with me, but they would take the literature that we handed out. Sadly, I never learned if any of these people ever came to faith. Some did attend what was called a "refugee" dinner. These dinners were held on a weekly basis, and the people would come to the mission to have a fine meal. Afterwards, the mission would try to find jobs for people who were out of work and would offer medical assistance to those who needed it. The people were very appreciative of the help that this Messianic organization was providing. The survivors of the Holocaust, who were often in a bad way, were most appreciative. It was awful to see the results of man's inhumanity to man, yet it was a blessing that we were able to meet some of their needs and show them the love of God.

Speaking Yiddish

The Old Brooklyn Mission, located at 590 Broadway and 27 Troop Avenue, was composed of mostly older Messianic Jews. They attended Tuesday and Friday night classes. I worked the Tuesday night class, serving refreshments. The meetings were usually done in the Russian language, and sometimes they would speak in Hebrew. They all spoke Yiddish, as was common for many Jews throughout the world. Yiddish is a language spoken by the

Ashkenazi (European) Jews. Yiddish was, and to some degree still is, the international language of Jewish people, no matter the country of residence. Beginning in the 10th century, Yiddish progressed from being a dialect of the German language to an independent language.

In addition to the heavy German influence, Yiddish is made up of Hebrew, Aramaic, Slavic, and Romance languages. The middle of the 1900s saw Yiddish slowly falling into disuse in the Jewish communities, especially in the United States.

I decided that things would go more smoothly for me if I learned some Yiddish. I was able to converse a little bit more by using Yiddish, and I even taught the people some Bible verses that I had learned in Yiddish. If I hadn't learned some Yiddish, I probably would never have been able to communicate with them. I wanted to be able to respond to their questions, so they would come to believe in Yeshua as their Messiah.

On Wednesdays, I was privileged to help another teacher who taught a women's class. This women's class consisted of Bible lessons and sewing lessons. The women were mostly older European Jewish women. I suggested that my fellow mission worker take a small number of these women as a separate group. She would work with the younger women who spoke English better than the older women. The women listened intently to the lessons and understood the message. They began to grow more and more in the Lord. I took the group of one dozen older Jewish ladies that spoke some English, but mostly Yiddish, since by this time I was somewhat functional in Yiddish. I said something about the New Testament, and the usual response that I received from one of the women was, "Oh, that Bible was written by the Goyim [Gentiles]." This was a tough group to reach with the Gospel.

The Dispensary

The Brooklyn Mission had a dispensary to serve the community's medical needs. On the wall of the dispensary, we had a sign that read:

This Dispensary is maintained by the
Williamsburg Mission to the Jews.
These are Christian people who love the
LORD JESUS CHRIST,
Our Messiah,
And they gave the money to carry on this work
So that you also may learn about this Messiah.
EVERY TRUE CHRISTIAN LOVES THE JEWS.

I would work in the dispensary in the Brooklyn Mission two days each week. This was where people came to see the doctor. When Leopold Cohn established the first mission, he knew that they had to help the people, most of whom were new immigrants to the U.S., to cope with life in a new land and culture. Part of this was providing medical services for little or no cost.

I was assigned to take the women's blood pressure, which was fine, except for the fact that I had no idea what I was doing. I had been shown how to take blood pressure just once and really hadn't learned a thing about it. My ignorance caused me to have a serious look on my face as I tried to figure out exactly how I was supposed to do this "blood pressure" thing. It was good that the women didn't know about my lack of knowledge because, if they saw my face, they might leave the clinic. As it was, they might think my somber look meant they had a health problem. They would nervously ask, "Am I okay? Is my blood pressure high?" They always seemed to feel better just knowing that someone cared about them. The usual charge for the clinic was twenty-five cents. Anyone from the neighborhood could come here for treatment or medical advice.

In 1946, people did not expect the type of medical care that is practiced today. This clinic was for minor aches and pains. Those who had a serious illness were referred to a clinic designed to treat serious illnesses. We had many brown glass jars containing pills of various colors. Unknown to the people, all of the bottles contained the same thing—aspirin. When the doctor saw a patient, he might prescribe a yellow pill for a minor ache or pain. If that didn't "cure" the symptoms, the person would return, and the doctor would say, "I have a stronger pill for you that should do the trick." He would turn to me and say, "Ruth, give this person a few green pills." I can't begin to tell you how many times this achieved positive results. The people would return home, telling of the great doctor they had in this clinic. I was tickled when this would happen, but I also learned another lesson. The human body is usually quite capable of healing itself in time, but the care and love given from one person to another has tremendous healing power.

On Thursdays and Fridays, I had more classes in Coney Island. This is how I got started in mission work. ABMJ gave me a schedule in three different locations. I really became familiar with the New York City subway system as a result. I worked hard and long hours and loved every minute of it. Why wouldn't I love this? I was doing the will of God, and that is exactly where I prayed to be every day of my life.

My Apartment

The room that I shared with Ceci served my purposes, but shortly after moving in, the city building inspector condemned the building and scheduled it to be torn down so they could build something new on that site. Ceci and I said goodbye to each other and went our separate ways. I moved into a small, one-room apartment next to a building where two other workers in the mission lived. The rent was five dollars per week, which was the same cost as the apartment I shared with Ceci. Since I earned $100 per month working for the mission, this place would do very nicely. I remember that it was a small room, only six or seven feet wide and about ten feet long. When I sat on my chair to read, my feet could reach the bed. There were three rooms on my floor, and we shared a common bathroom.

Living in New York was quite an interesting experience for a young girl from Ontario. I remember the woman who was in the room next to mine. Once, when she was going to be away for a weekend, she asked me if I would do her a favor. She had arranged for someone to spray her room for bugs and asked me to sweep out her apartment after that person left. I said that I would do this for her. When I opened the door to her room, I felt as if I was looking at every roach in the world. The room was covered with dead roaches.

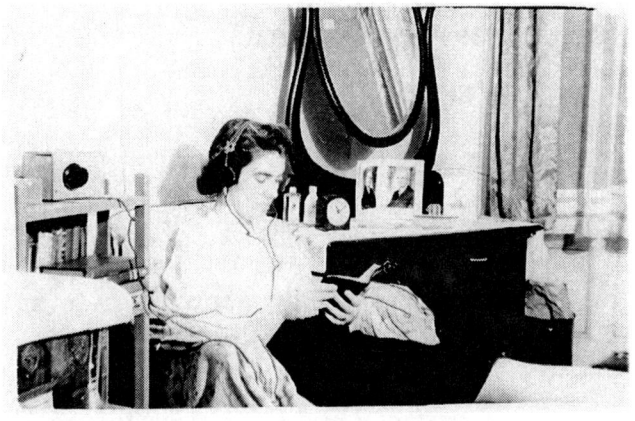

Ruth Studying in Her Small Apartment, 1946

I swept them up and disposed of them. I always wondered why I never saw a roach in my room since this woman seemed to have such a great population living in her room. I guess it was a miracle that kept these bugs away. However, I did have to deal with bedbugs—another new experience for me in New York.

My Neighbors—Holocaust Survivors

I started working for ABMJ on October 1, 1946. The ministry had been in existence for over fifty years at that point and had suffered much persecution from Jews and Christians alike. Despite attempts to stop ABMJ's work, the mission succeeded and grew. The year of 1946 posed a problem the mission had never faced before. I came on the scene just one year after the end of World War II. The Jews in the neighborhood had either lost relatives in the Nazi Holocaust or they were actually survivors of the death camps in Europe.

Just down the hall from the apartment I was renting in Borough Park lived a Jewish couple who had survived the Holocaust. These lovely people would wait for me to come home at night from my work at the mission so that we could sit and talk for a while. They enjoyed my company and the conversations we had together. The times I spent with them taught me much about the Jewish people, and I heard firsthand of the sufferings they had experienced. They had owned a factory in Germany, which had been taken from them by the Nazi government. Even worse, all of their family perished in the camps. They told me about their terrifying experiences. This couple had been scarred emotionally as well as physically by the brutal treatment they had witnessed and endured. I heard their words but could only imagine the atrocities they had suffered. They explained how they had developed certain desperate practices that allowed them to survive when so many millions of others did not.

One of the things they did to survive occurred in winter. They were often required to stand for hours outside their barracks in the bone-chilling cold. Their skin would freeze. When they came back inside, where there was fire, they learned to stay away from the warm fire until their bodies had gradually warmed up. If they did not, their frozen skin would peel off, causing great pain. This also caused severe infection, which could be fatal in the concentration camps.

When I shared how sad I was that they had lost the factory they had worked so hard to build, they said, "We can always get another factory, but we can never get any of our family members back again." I was just a young girl, but that statement seared itself into my memory, and I never forgot it. Through that exchange, God taught me that it wasn't *things* that were important, but it was always the *people* who were important.

This couple was very kind and loving, and the time we spent together seemed to benefit them as much as it did me. The wife was not a good sleeper and would often wake up quite early in the morning. Her first order of business was to take a bath. The bathroom was a hall bathroom that served the three one-room apartments on the second floor. The plumbing was situated in the walls in such a way that the pipes leading to the bathtub shared the same wall where the head of my bed was located. This dear woman did not want the noise of running water to awaken me, so she would take wash cloths and wrap them around the faucet so the sound of the running water was muffled, and I could enjoy my sleep uninterrupted. To this day, I am still amazed that this woman, who had been through such a terrible existence, would consider my need for sleep and take the necessary action to ensure that I was not disturbed. Her caring and kindness made a great impression on me. Here was a daughter of Abraham, a Jewish woman, showing the love of God to a young Christian woman.

The lesson that I learned was that no matter what I was going through, I should not be bitter. I learned that I needed to remain kind and loving. God used these people to teach me about the people that I needed to relate to, as well to teach me about how I should live my life. I am thankful that God allowed me to share Messiah with them on many different occasions, despite the fact that they had a difficult time hearing the Gospel. This was understandable since they had been persecuted by so-called "Christians" during the Holocaust.

This couple was just one of many messengers God sent my way to teach and encourage me.

The Coney Island Mission

I worked for eight years in the Coney Island Mission. Coney Island is a long narrow island at the southern tip of Brooklyn. It has wonderful beaches on the Atlantic Ocean and is a fantastic area for recreation.

When I first came to the Coney Island Mission on October 1, I didn't even have a clue as to why the people in the mission were wishing me a Happy New Year. Why would anyone do that on October 1? I wondered if they were reading their calendars correctly. I was so unfamiliar with the Jewish culture that I was not aware that Rosh Hashanah, the Jewish New Year, occurred at that time.

Our mission building was a two-story building with people living upstairs. These were Messianic Jewish people who took care of the building. The main level had a room that we used as a meeting place. There was also a long narrow basement where I worked with the children.

Coney Island Mission

Soon, I was teaching a boys' class and a girls' class of local children after school. These children would attend public school and come to my class after school at 3 p.m. Quite often the situation was such that, at first, the children would attend the mission, but the parents would not. However, in many cases, the parents eventually did come to mission activities.

I would teach the children's Bible classes and handicrafts, where I would show them how to make paper airplanes. They also played games, on occasion. I eventually was given the larger classes of teenagers. They all had a great time in these classes. Not all of the children were believers, but every child was required to have permission from a parent to attend. I recall one parent who told her little girl, "If they say the name of Jesus, put your hands over your ears." I can still remember this girl slapping her hands over her ears whenever she heard the name of Jesus. I do not think that she attended for too long a period of time. If we had admitted a child without written permission, we would have had a lot of trouble on our hands.

In the late 1940s and early 1950s at the Coney Island Mission, there was a lot of opposition from the local Jewish population, since a lot of Jewish people were accepting Jesus, Yeshua, as their Messiah. One day, shortly after I began working there, I was walking down the street. One of the local people came up and spit on me because I was teaching the Jewish children about Jesus. This occurred early in my time at Coney Island, and I still did not know enough about Jewish people to understand why someone would spit on me simply because I told them about the Messiah. There was a lot more opposition from the Jewish community back then than there is today.

On another occasion, the entire neighborhood seemed to rise up in rebellion against the mission. More than once, a young rabbi from one of the local synagogues stood at the gate at the entrance to the mission center. Hilda Koser would boldly go out to the front gate to confront him. She would instruct the women arriving for class to ignore this man who was telling them not to enter. He would say, "Don't go in there. These people want to convert you to become Christians." To my knowledge, no one was ever influenced by this rabbi.

There were children's classes and women's Bible classes, but the mission did not hold Sunday services when I first arrived. However, shortly after I arrived, a man named Dr. Heydt began a Sunday morning worship service. It was well-accepted and well-attended. The people who came to the mission usually did not attend a regular religious service, since the synagogues wanted nothing to do with them, and they did not feel comfortable attending a church. If a family wanted a child to become Bar Mitzvah (Jewish confirmation at age thirteen), they had no choice but to go to a synagogue. This could be troublesome for the family because most synagogues would not allow a thirteen-year-old to become Bar Mitzvah if he believed in Jesus.

In Hilda Koser's autobiography *Come and Get It*, she describes the problems with a Jewish believer who wants to have a Bar Mitzvah. This excerpt describes the father of a young man who came to Hilda Koser to ask for help in arranging a Bar Mitzvah for his son.

When the oldest son, Albert, was almost thirteen years of age, the father came to the mission for the first time. "My son wants a Bar Mitzvah (confirmation), but my wife won't let him go to the synagogue. Speak with her; she listens to you."

I was surprised and asked Albert, "Why do you want to go to the synagogue?

"All my friends have parties and get presents," he answered.

"Oh, is that what you want? A party and presents? I'll make you one." Turning to the father, I said, "It might be a little different, for he will be reading not only from the Old Testament, but also from the New. His mother will give a testimony as to her faith in Jesus (Yeshua), the Messiah. There will be a special speaker, and we'll present Albert with a whole Bible. Then we will have a big party. I will send invitations to all our people, and they will bring presents."

The father couldn't believe that I would go to all this bother for his son, and he gave his consent. It was unheard of in those days for anyone to have a Hebrew-Christian Bar Mitzvah, but we had one, and it was a beautiful affair. We even had the children throw little packages of raisins and almonds, which is a traditional orthodox custom."

During my years at the Coney Island Mission, it was a joy to see a great number of Jewish children and adults profess faith in Jesus as their Messiah. Praise the Lord!

Gentile Evangelism of Jewish People

Believe it or not, it was easier for a Gentile to reach Jewish people than it was for a Jewish believer to do so. The reason for this is that the Jewish believer is seen as a traitor to the Jewish faith. I was not from a Jewish background, and where I lived in Canada, I did not even have much exposure to the Jewish culture. When we worked with the Jewish people of Brooklyn, we taught them the Messianic prophecies, how Jesus is the fulfillment of the Jewish holidays, and traditional hymns. One of the Jewish people's favorite hymns to sing was "What A Friend We Have In Jesus." They wanted to know what we knew. They didn't need to hear things from a Jewish perspective. They already had a Jewish identity, which gave them a Jewish perspective. So, what made this type of evangelism Jewish? The people made it Jewish. Since they were all Jewish, they brought their Jewishness to our evangelism. Most of the women that I interacted with were Orthodox or Conservative Jews who had come to faith in their Messiah, Yeshua, Jesus. At the mission, there were mostly Jewish people in attendance. This was the source of the ministry's Jewishness.

Brooklyn Gathering—Jewish Children, 1951

In Coney Island, a typical scenario went like this: Twelve Jewish believers would attend mission activities. They would then bring twelve friends who were unbelieving Jews. This meant that there were now twenty-four attending. This increase was not really due to the mission workers' going out into the Jewish community, although door-to-door evangelism did take place. We didn't have to do this in Coney Island because the people in the neighborhood knew we were there and knew who we were, so we didn't have to introduce ourselves. It is interesting to note that the opposition we received from the rabbis helped to spread the word that we were there.

CHAPTER 6
Mission Work

Most missions had nothing much going in the years before the late 1960s until the early 1970s. Daniel Fuchs used to say that he knew every Jewish Christian in the country because there weren't very many of them in those years. There just wasn't very much happening in the missions. It was said as a joke that, when one mission would have a Jew come to faith, they would write and tell of this salvation. They would then send this article to the other missions. The other missions would change the name of the person who had been saved and write it up in their newsletter as if they had seen a different person come to faith. There seemed to be so few new believers in those years.

ABMJ was the largest mission to the Jews in the years of the 1940s and 1950s. They had an ongoing missionary work that was productive when there were not the masses of Jewish people coming to faith as had occurred in previous decades. The focus of the mission in the 1940s, '50s, and '60s was on second-generation Jewish people who were born in this country, not recently-arrived immigrants, whose numbers had decreased tremendously.

In the 1950s, I was working in Manhattan and Brooklyn. I had heard that there was going to be a conference sponsored by other missions to the Jewish people. At that time, ABMJ was one of the largest and most successful missions. We were active and still growing in the number of Jewish people who came to our facilities. There was not a lot of interaction between the missions that were reaching out to the Jewish people with the Good News of Jesus. I felt that it would be a great idea if I attended this conference. I approached my friend and fellow worker, Eleanor Bullock, and we went to this conference. I remember walking down this long aisle to a few available seats. I could feel all eyes on us, as no one knew who we were. We had the opportunity to speak with many of the workers in other missions. This eventually led to an increase in communication and interaction between the different missions. This also directly influenced the establishment of The Fellowship of Christian Testimonies to the Jews, an organization made up of the various Jewish and Gentile ministries working with the Jewish people. There was a real need for all of the workers in the mission field to have fellowship and to share their experiences, successes, and failures. Mostly, we were able to work together to advance the Gospel to the Jewish people. This was a very successful organization that sadly no longer exists.

Hilda Koser

LINEAGE—Five generations of Messianic believers who became believers through the work of ABMJ.

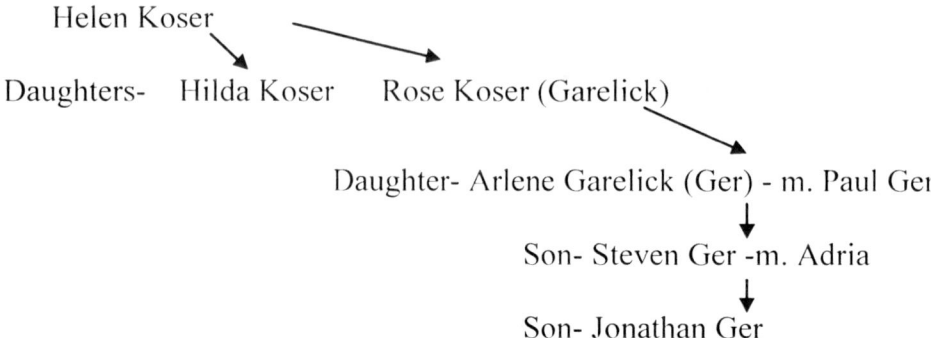

Helen Koser

Daughters-   Hilda Koser   Rose Koser (Garelick)

Daughter- Arlene Garelick (Ger) - m. Paul Ger

Son- Steven Ger -m. Adria

Son- Jonathan Ger

Hilda Koser and Ruth, 1947

Hilda Koser spent all of her years in ministry working at the Coney Island Mission station of the American Board of Missions to the Jews/Chosen People Ministries. Hilda was a second-generation Messianic Jew. Her mother, Helen Koser, was a Jewish believer. Hilda's sister, Rose was also a believer. Hilda Koser eventually became the director of the Coney Island Mission. The Coney Island Mission was her love and her life. She was very protective of the people at the mission, and she cared deeply for them. She thought of the people at the mission as her "angels." Hilda was a wonderful missionary who had an evangelistic heart. She was a wonderful teacher and eagerly shared the Gospel and Messianic prophecy with Jewish people. Her family had come to know the Lord through the ministry of Miss Augusta Sussdorf.

Many of the women who came to the Coney Island Mission were from an Orthodox Jewish background. Hilda would always take special time to share the Gospel with these women. There were services on the weekend as well as a Sunday School program. When I started at Coney Island, we had just one building. Shortly thereafter, they enlarged the facility by acquiring the building right next door. They took down the wall between the two buildings and expanded it into one larger building. This also provided a bigger basement to work in for all of the programs that the mission was running. This was very helpful.

Hilda had been working at the mission for a few years and had never been on a long trip. At the beginning of 1947, she very much wanted to go on a trip to Israel (which was not established as an independent nation until May 1948). Hilda wanted to go—and she did. I had been working at the mission for only three months, and I was left in charge. This was an interesting time in my career and in my life. I didn't really know what I was doing. I hadn't even learned much about Jewish culture and customs. Now, I found myself in a leadership position when I hadn't yet fully learned how to follow. I believe that it was only because of my God-given adventuresome spirit that I rose to the challenge and embraced this daunting task. To this very day, I believe that if God gives me something to do, He will give me the ability to successfully achieve it. Hilda shortened her trip because she became lonely for her people that she ministered to at the mission. I was glad to see her come home.

Hilda was most influential when it came to the teaching she provided to the people who attended classes. She was an excellent teacher because she knew her people so well that she knew precisely what they needed and wanted to know. Among the many topics that she taught were Messianic prophecy, Jesus in the Old Testament, and the holidays with Jesus as the Passover Lamb of God. The people in her classes were really well-educated. The teaching of Jesus in the Old Testament cut through most of the inbred resistance that the Jewish people had to hearing the Good News of what their Messiah had done for them. I learned from Hilda many things that she had learned about teaching. I also learned how to present Jesus to the children in such a way that they would understand Him and accept His message.

Christmas Programs

When I first started at the mission, Christmas programs were the big thing. Hilda was very particular about having her children dressed up as shepherds and wise men, etc. The mission would invite the entire neighborhood to come to this Christmas event. This was the 1950s, and we would pack the mission full of Jewish people. We would have between 100 and 120 people attending. That was an amazing number to have in attendance. In those days, we did not celebrate the Passover or Rosh Hashanah the way it is done today. The favorite song of the people in the Coney Island Mission was "What A Friend We Have In Jesus." Back in that era, we taught the people Messianic prophecies. Everything we taught had Jesus as the focus of the lesson. Looking back these many years, in some ways, I prefer that type of teaching. In that time, all the missions followed this way of presenting Christmas and Resurrection Sunday (Easter) by honoring the Messiah, Jesus. We taught the Jewish Holy Days, such as Passover, but we didn't have a community celebration of Passover at the mission back then. Today, we tend to see missions and congregations that do one or the other. I believe that the way to do it is to combine the two with Jesus at the center of them all.

I don't see the type of spiritual growth today that we had in those days with Hilda. Her women grew and loved the Lord. They learned Scriptures and sang songs about their Messiah. They fell in love with Jesus. That is missing today. Hilda was very much in love with her Messiah, and it showed. She loved her people and would go to extremes to teach and assist them. As a result, Hilda saw a lot of fruit. Many children and adults came to faith through the mission in Coney Island.

Hilda Koser was instrumental in Michael Rydelnik's coming to know the Lord. Today, Dr. Rydelnik is a highly respected Professor of Jewish Studies at Moody Bible Institute. Hilda spent over a year going over all the Messianic prophecies with young Michael. This teaching was very influential in Michael's accepting Jesus as his Lord and Savior.

After nearly forty years of service, Hilda eventually took a one-year sabbatical from the mission. She went to Florida for the year. When she was ready to return, she discovered that Chosen People Ministries had assigned someone else to run the mission in Coney Island. The mission, understandably, needed to have someone to run it on a constant basis. One year is a long time not to have consistent leadership because, in a one-year period, many things change. Even so, it was sad that Hilda never had the chance to come back from Florida to say goodbye to her people.

I enjoyed my time working with Hilda at the mission. I worked in Coney Island for the first eight years of my career from October 1946 to late 1954.

Helen Koser—The Matriarch of the Koser Family

At this point, I would like to share the story of Hilda Koser's mother, Helen Koser. At ABMJ/CPM, we had many responsibilities. One of my responsibilities was to visit those who were ill. One of those people was Helen Koser, Hilda Koser's mother. She was a fervent believer in Messiah, Jesus, and had paid a great price for her belief. However, her faith was strong and never wavered. I visited her in the hospital because she was quite sick and in the final stages of cancer. She did not have long to live. Sometimes, before I would make a visit to an ill person, I would go to the store to pick up something to bring. It was amazing to see how a small item could brighten a sick person's day. This day, I had stopped and bought something for Mrs. Koser.

I entered her room and greeted her, and she said to me, "Miss Wardell, I know what you have in that brown bag." This took me by surprise as I wondered how she could know that. She continued, "I have been praying that God would send me an orange, so I know that is what you have in that bag." It was an impossibility that she could have known what was in that plain brown paper bag. The fact of the matter was that I *did* have oranges in the bag. I quickly took one out and peeled it for her. She enjoyed that immensely. I spent some time with Mrs. Koser, and as I left her room, I understood that when one prays correctly, one should have faith that God will answer that prayer. I was just a young missionary, and the lesson I learned that day blessed me greatly and is something that has stayed with me all of my life.

Hilda's mother passed away shortly after my visit, and it was interesting to note that, while Helen Koser was a strong believer in Jesus, some of her family members were not. The family was Jewish, but all had not received the Jewish Messiah, Yeshua, Jesus. Helen Koser was buried in a Jewish cemetery. In the Jewish tradition, there is an "unveiling service" no later than eleven months after the funeral. At that time, the headstone is uncovered. For Helen, the unveiling service arrangements were made by family members who were not believers in Jesus. A rabbi from one of the local synagogues was asked to officiate at the unveiling service. The people attending from the mission, who knew and loved Mrs. Koser, along with members of the family, were on the verge of tears. This sadness lasted until the rabbi showed up. Much to our surprise, the rabbi who came to lead the service was none other than the same rabbi who had just recently confronted Hilda at the front gate to the mission in Coney Island (see p. 38). Most of the people in the crowd recognized this rabbi, and that is when the visible sadness disappeared. When he saw Hilda there at the graveside, he looked somewhat shocked and said to Hilda, "I know you." The crowd looked on in anticipation of what might happen next, but thankfully the service took place with no unusual interruptions.

When I first came to the Brooklyn Mission, some of the Koser family were attending the mission activities. Arlene Garelick was then about fifteen years old. Her mother Rose attended the meetings on a regular basis. Hilda Koser, of course, was present because she worked for the mission. There was a third Koser sister, Milly, who was a believer and lived out on Long Island with her two children, whom I worked with. As a result, I had quite a bit of contact with the Koser family.

Arlene Garelick

Arlene Garelick was the daughter of Rose (Koser) Garelick, the sister of Hilda Koser. That made Arlene, Hilda's niece and Helen Koser's granddaughter. She was a third generation Jewish believer and a person who was always pleasant to be with. Arlene grew up, moved out of town to New Jersey, and married Paul Ger. After that I did not see her a lot. She sometimes attended special events at the Coney Island Mission, and I would see her then. I always loved Arlene. She was from the "old school" where we sang hymns, held Christmas

**Arlene Garelick –
Camp 1946**

programs, etc. In her later years, she planned to come to the Dallas-Fort Worth area from New Jersey to be near her only child, Steven, who was living there after having moved to Dallas to attend Dallas Theological Seminary. I had moved to Texas in 1993.

When Arlene informed me that she was moving from New Jersey to the Dallas area, I was very excited. Arlene had been one of my campers back in 1947 – 1948. She was our best all-around camper one year. She was a vivacious, warm, happy person, and I was very fond of her. By this point in her life, Arlene was dealing with many health problems. I often visited her in the hospital, and on a few occasions, we got to "really" share some of our experiences of days gone by. We didn't have much time together, because not long after moving to Texas, the Lord took her home. However, even in that short period of time, we had an opportunity to share with each other, and that time was very special to me.

Arlene's husband, Paul Ger, was Jewish, but not a believer. The day that Arlene died, Paul Ger became a believer in the Lord. Today he lives near his son, Steven, and attends a Messianic Congregation in Dallas. Steven is now in ministry in Texas. He is married and has a son, Jonathan, who has also accepted Jesus as his Lord. That is five generations of Jewish believers from the Koser family.

Steven Ger—Son of Arlene (Garelick) Ger

Steven Ger

Steve is a fourth-generation Messianic believer. I didn't know much about Steve when he was a child, since he was in New York, and I was in California at that time. He was in college when his great-aunt, Hilda Koser, passed away. It was about this time that I would send some financial support for him. I really got to know him when I moved to the Dallas area in 1993.

After his graduation from seminary, Steve established Sojourner's Ministries, a teaching ministry. I served on the Board of Directors for nine or ten years. I was blessed to see his ministry grow from the beginning to the present time. I really got to know him as a teacher and a *kibbitzer* (Yiddish for one who likes to talk). He is also an author and a wonderful, talented musician. I saw him marry and have a son. I came to love his family, and now I have the opportunity to teach his son Jonathan in preparation for his Bar Mitzvah. Jonathan is the fifth generation of this family that I have known personally. This included Steve, his mother, grandmother, and his great-grandmother. Steve is a joy because of his great desire to serve the Lord.

Steven Ger's Memories

My story is unique in that I am a fourth generation Jewish believer. My mother was a believer, but my father was not. [*Editor's note*: Steve's dad, Paul, has since come to faith.] My great-grandmother, Helen Koser, was an immigrant to the United States who had eight children. Due to my great-grandfather's health issues, Helen was left to raise her children by herself. She would avail herself of the services provided by the American Board of Missions to the Jews, such as medical clinics. The mission workers also held

Steve Ger, Arlene, Hilda Koser, Sylvia, and Rose

classes to teach English to new arrivals, as well as classes to provide people with the skills to secure jobs. At the medical clinic, the workers invited my great-grandmother to come to a class to hear about the Messiah in the Yiddish language. She attended and brought along some of her children, and in time, she became a believer in Jesus—as did her daughter Rose (my grandmother) and her other daughters Hilda, Sylvia, and Milly (my great-aunts).

Helen's daughter Hilda worked closely with Ruth in Coney Island. My grandmother Rose had a daughter, Arlene (my mother), who was one of Ruth's campers. My son Jonathan, a fifth-generation Jewish believer, has begun receiving Bar Mitzvah lessons from Ruth. It is a great blessing for me to see the circle that began with my great-grandmother come to closure with my son being trained for his Bar Mitzvah by Ruth Wardell. This is a unique relationship in that Ruth is the ministerial link between five generations of my family.

Steve Remembers—The Retreats

My early memories of Ruth span the years of 1971 to 1973. I only saw Ruth once each year at retreats. Ruth was such great fun. All of the kids had heard that she was fun, and we all had a great time with her. The retreats that were offered to the young people had to be earned. To qualify, I had to memorize a specified number of Bible verses. I recall that we drove for several hours out into the countryside to some hotel with a nice lake. In addition to teaching great Bible lessons, Ruth did stuff like short-sheeting beds, playing practical jokes on the kids, and shooting us with water guns. Those were great times for me.

In my adult years, she supported me in my studies and in starting Sojourner Ministries. She became a valued advisor. Upon Aunt Hilda's death in December of 1994, Ruth, in one sense, became the repository for all of my family history in that she knew four generations of my family. Ruth was indeed a link to my heritage. She became a source of wisdom as well as a blessing. I could share with her all of my joys as well as my frustrations with the modern Messianic Movement. She provided a sympathetic ear and advice as to which direction I should go.

When I started Sojourner Ministries in 1996, she agreed to be on my Board of Directors. She served on the Board until 2006. She was also a source of tremendous encouragement in what was, at times, a sea of discouragement. When I was starting out, just hearing Ruth's approval to go ahead was sufficient enough for me to have confidence in what I was doing.

Ruth has seen countless Messianic fads come and has also seen most of them go—and then come back around again. It is significant that she had the experience to know that those ideas were bad back then and that they are still bad ideas today. This helped me to avoid many problems in carrying out the work of Sojourner Ministries. Ruth is known and respected throughout the Messianic Movement, and she knows most of the leaders in the movement today. Some have even been her "kids" from the past.

The programs that Ruth and my Aunt Hilda ran for the youth came to an end when they retired from the mission. It is difficult to find any programs like that for children and adults in the Messianic Movement today.

Ruth was strategically placed because she had a good attitude. She could be great fun at one point, but at another point, she would tolerate no nonsense. She was very straightforward with the people that she ministered to, and this is something sorely missing in the current missions.

The philosophy of ABMJ was that if you had a responsibility, and you made it work, you stayed. It was a tough, no-nonsense world, where if you did something untoward, you were out. It was a tough world because Jewish mission work was tough. It was not for the faint of heart or for the thin-skinned. Joseph Hoffman Cohn was tough when he had to be. The history of the mission and the troubles that he and his father, Leopold Cohn, had to go through made them tough in order to survive. This influenced my aunt and Ruth. Basically, you sank or swam. Obviously, both my aunt and Ruth learned how to swim quite well.

Michael Rydelnik—Memories

[*Editor's note*: Dr. Michael Rydelnik is Professor of Jewish Studies at the Moody Bible Institute in Chicago, Illinois. He is the son of Holocaust survivors. Michael was raised in an Orthodox Jewish home in Brooklyn, New York. He has a diploma in Jewish Studies from Moody Bible Institute, a bachelor's degree in Biblical Literature from Azusa Pacific University, and a Master of Theology in New Testament Literature and Exegesis from Dallas Theological Seminary. He did his doctoral studies in Intercultural Studies at Trinity Evangelical Divinity School. Dr. Rydelnik is the author of several books.]

Ruth and Michael Rydelnik, 2007

I've known Ruth since I was fifteen years old. I was part of Hilda Koser's youth group in Coney Island. There was a youth group in Hollis, Queens, that met on Friday night. This meeting was run by Ruth Wardell. It was an interesting experience because Ruth had a youth group that was really hopping. There was a Bible study out in the garage for the young people. Ruth was teaching the younger group. Bill and Jo Ennis were teaching the adults. I really wasn't under Ruth's teaching since she was with the younger children. What I do remember is that I used to hang around with her afterward.

One of the things that really struck me was Ruth's very interesting balance of commitment to teaching the truth and a tolerance for people who disagreed with her. She was a person who could teach the truth and not be irritable or an irritant. I really appreciated that. While Ruth didn't seem to mind rock and roll, we always would sing hymns when we were in the car with her.

My second impression of Ruth occurred at my house. Ruth was visiting my house with one of the girls in the group named Sandy Schoenblum. On that particular day, the rabbi from the Yeshiva was on his way over because he had heard that my family had become believers in Christ. He wanted to find out what in the world was going on. When the rabbi arrived, I witnessed this most interesting scene. The rabbi is standing there with his great beard, and here is this Gentile woman, Ruth, whom I thought would be greatly intimidated by this man of God. It immediately became clear to me that Ruth was not the least bit intimidated. I also remember that even though Ruth was bold and direct, the rabbi was not offended.

Ruth was always taking us on trips. We would go canoeing in New Jersey. Ruth would load up two vans with kids and head out. She would drive the van down the highway with her knees while her hands were in the air as she led the group in a song. We didn't need the radio.

We would just sing songs about Jesus. My earliest memories of Ruth were of a person who was bold, yet tolerant and understanding.

Ruth has always been my greatest encourager. When I was going through some medical issues, Ruth encouraged me through my recovery. The mission and Ruth provided a place where believing Jewish children could go and feel safe. I and my fellow believers were often isolated from our families, neighbors, and friends because of our faith. The youth groups led by Hilda and Ruth at the mission gave us the fellowship that we sorely needed. I went to camp many summers when I otherwise would not have gone. Each individual mission station was not that large. When the children from many mission stations got together for retreats or camp, there were 100 to 150 children who got to spend time with like-minded people. In those days, almost all of the children at camp were Jewish believers. What I will remember the most is that we always had a great time whenever we got together.

CHAPTER 7
Leaving Coney Island

It was 1954. Eight years had passed since I had come to the mission. I believed in my heart and in my spirit that God was directing me to move on from the Coney Island Mission. I believed that He wanted me to start a new season in my mission life. My father was a church planter back in Canada, and he was always starting a new work. I inherited this desire from my father. I left Coney Island and went to help establish mission stations in Queens and Long Island. I also worked in the Old Williamsburg Mission in Brooklyn.

Eleanor Bullock

Eleanor Bullock came from a small town in Pennsylvania and attended a Bible college in Binghamton, New York. She felt the call of God to go into Jewish missions, and she came to ABMJ in 1945, less than one year before I arrived. When I arrived in 1946, we were both very young, and we didn't know much about what we were doing. One thing we had in common was that we were both very tall. We worked closely together, and we were quite compatible.

Eleanor Bullock and Ruth, 1948

No matter what ministry we worked in, our paths crossed on a weekly basis. She had been working for the mission with a class of older Orthodox Jewish women. The mission put me there to help Eleanor with this class. Some of the women were believers, and some weren't. They did enjoy the sewing class that the mission offered in the afternoon. These were Jewish women who spoke a lot of Yiddish. When I left Coney Island and started out to build mission stations in Queens and Long Island, we worked together. Eleanor worked the Women's Meetings (Bible studies), and I worked the Children's Meetings in Levittown, Huntington Station, and Flushing.

In addition to working very closely with Eleanor, we spent some of our vacations together. We went to Israel with Arnold Fruchtenbaum for our twenty-fifth anniversary with the mission. Arnold served as our tour guide in 1971.

Eleanor worked her entire career for ABMJ/CPM in New York City. She was a dear friend for over fifty years before the Lord took her home in July 2002. She was a wonderful missionary who loved the Lord. She was known for her tremendous Bible teaching. People really learned the Scriptures when they sat in Eleanor's class. I still miss her. I often wish that I could call her on the phone to speak about what is happening in CPM today.

We had also started a station in East New York, Brooklyn, which lasted for just one year. It was during this year in East New York that the Fruchtenbaum family was contacted, and Arnold Fruchtenbaum came and accepted Jesus as his Messiah.

Arnold Fruchtenbaum

[*Editor's note*: Arnold G. Fruchtenbaum, Th.M., Ph.D., is one of the foremost authorities on the nation of Israel and is a Messianic Jewish believer. This has made him a popular speaker and teacher for Bible conferences, congregations, and churches throughout the world. He is the founder and director of Ariel Ministries, which is dedicated to the evangelism of Jewish people and the discipleship of Jewish and Gentile believers from a Messianic Jewish frame of reference. He has been married for over forty years to the former Mary Ann Morrow.]

Ruth's Comments

Dr. Arnold Fruchtenbaum has quite an impressive resume; however, I met him back when he was twelve years old, when everyone knew him as just "Arnold."

The Early Days with Arnold Fruchtenbaum and How He Came to Faith

I first met Arnold Fruchtenbaum when I knocked on his family's door. I had received his address card from ABMJ in New York. His mother had filled out this address card some six years previously and had left it with Dr. Daniel Fuchs. New arrivals to America moved frequently, so it would have been a rare thing for us to find a family still in the same place after six years had passed. I followed up on this address, not expecting to find the family. We didn't know the Fruchtenbaums, and I didn't have any idea of who they were. When I went to the apartment, I met Arnold's mother. who did not speak a lot of English. I explained to her that I had gotten the card from ABMJ in New York. When I asked her if I could pick up

Arnold, his sister, and his brother, to bring them to the mission center for activities, she gave me permission. I found out later that she thought we were a Jewish organization, which, in fact, we were. She felt that if the children went to the classes with me that we would help them.

The children came into my class. When Arnold heard what we were teaching, he was not happy with the subject matter. We were teaching that Jesus was the Jewish Messiah. I gave him a New Testament to take home and read that week, rather than trying to answer all his questions. He didn't know a thing about the New Testament. He also did not

Arnold—12th Birthday

know or understand why we believed in Jesus. He was determined that the next time he came to the class, he would prove us wrong, so he went home and read the New Testament. The more he read, the more he realized how Jewish the New Testament really was. When he came back the following week, he was more ready and open to listen to what was being taught.

When I went home after that first class, I found my Isaac Leeser Bible. Isaac Leeser was a rabbi who had translated the Old Testament from Hebrew into English. I felt that by having this Bible with me, I would have a lot to share with Arnold. My intuition was correct. I wrote down all of the page numbers so that I could quickly find the Messianic prophecies, since in the Jewish Bible, the books are arranged in a different order from the Old Testament in the Christian Bible. I went through all the prophecies, and I can still see the list in my head. These Scriptures covered the topics of the birth, life, death, and resurrection of Jesus. I showed Arnold all of the prophecies about Jesus in the Isaac Leeser Bible. Arnold considered the Leeser version a "kosher" Bible. I never knew that Isaac Leeser was such an important person to Jewish people. I just happened to have this Bible in my library. Arnold had diligently read the New Testament, and he had a better idea of who Jesus was, so as I pointed out these Messianic Scriptures in the Old Testament, he was able to match those prophecies up with the fulfillment that took place in the New Testament. The second time he came to the class, Arnold accepted Jesus as his Messiah.

Arnold became an ardent believer and began to study on his own. He would meet people and witness to them. He would give me a list of the names of people that he witnessed to so I could follow up in my role as a worker for ABMJ. I found it quite interesting that a young boy had such presence of mind. I picked him up each week, and we would study together. Since the East New York station was only recently opened, there were not a lot of young people for Arnold to meet. It was only on the retreats when he would meet up with students his own age. Looking back, I understand now why he looked forward so much to these retreats. To me, it was just another retreat. However, for Arnold, this was something that was very important in his life.

Our retreats were at a place where there was really nothing much to do except what we planned for ourselves. Arnold used to prepare questions related to the Bible for our time of recreation. At the first or second retreat that we went on, I asked Arnold if he would say a word to the group. Not only did he speak a word, he masterfully went through the Book of Job. We all sat there and listened intently, flabbergasted because we did not really understand how much he knew about the Bible at the young age of thirteen. It was his first sermon, and it was very wonderful. Of course, today, Dr. Arnold Fruchtenbaum is a well-known theologian and scholar, but to us, at that time, he was just Arnold.

In the *Newspaper of Long Island Teenagers*, January-February of 1958, Arnold wrote his first article about prayer.

Prayer

By Arnold Fruchtenbaum

Prayer is a wonderful thing. You'd be surprised to see the things that could be done by it.

Jesus, Himself, told us to pray. But you must know how to do it to get good results. Now suppose you decided to ask God for a bike which you wanted very badly. This is the way you should not go about it.

"Dear God, now You know that I want a bike, and since I am praying for it, and I believe in You, You should give me one, Amen."

This is absolutely the way not to pray. In order to pray, you must remember two things—ask God if it's His will and end the prayer in Jesus' name.

This reminds me of a woman who didn't ask God's will to be done.

As the story goes, this woman had a son who was dying. Since no doctor could save him, she started to pray, and she prayed for hours, "God save my son, let my son live."

When her friends told her that she was not praying for God's will to be done but her own, she said she didn't care as long as her son lived.

Well, God granted her wish, and her son lived—only to die in the electric chair. So because she prayed the wrong way, her son, who should've gone to Heaven, went to Hell.

Let's go back to the bike now. Here is the right way to pray for it:

"Dear Heavenly Father, I now pray that if it is Thy will, thou shalt give me some way to get a bike. I pray it in Jesus' name, Amen."

Do not expect God to answer all your prayers. He may answer only some of them—those that He knows should be granted to you.

Now you may ask me how I know that God answers prayer. Well, once God answered one of my prayers, which I will never forget.

For one year now, I have kept this a secret. Only one other person in the world knows about it, Miss Ruth Wardell. But now I am ready to share this with everyone else.

It happened at Christmas Eve in 1956. I was reading the Bible and I came across the part that tells about the star which shone over Bethlehem the night Jesus was born. After I finished reading, I hoped very much to see the star. So I prayed to God that if it was His will, He would let me see that same star.

I prayed all night with no results. Finally, still looking at the sky, I fell asleep and dreamed a most wonderful dream, in which I saw a very beautiful star. When I awoke, I knew in my heart God answered my prayer, as I pray He may yours, through Jesus Christ, our Lord.

Arnold never missed a retreat. However, he *almost* missed one, which he wrote about in an article for our group newspaper in March of 1958. The article is reprinted below.

Answered Prayer

By Arnold Fruchtenbaum

For months now, since I came home from the November Retreat, I couldn't wait until February 21, the date set for the next one. I was dying for that weekend to get here, and counted the days off, one by one.

I saved as much money as possible, and had been practicing this song for months on my violin for the special weekend. My violin had a crack in it, and I saved enough money to get it fixed. I even tried to get new strings for it.

Arnold Fruchtenbaum – Violinist

But then—kaplunk—on that Sunday before that special weekend, the biggest snowstorm in years hit the city, and I began to get worried that the trip would be canceled. So I did the only thing that could possibly help. I prayed.

On Wednesday, my father told me that no matter what happened, I would not be able to go. So again, I prayed.

Then, on Wednesday night, I called Miss Wardell and asked her if the trip was canceled. She said it hadn't been. To make sure, she told me that she would call me up on Thursday.

My father was afraid that the roads would be too icy. So again, I prayed, and asked God that if it was His will, He would somehow, provide a way for me to go.

Just as she had promised, Miss Wardell called me up and said that the trip was still on.

My father still hadn't changed his mind, even though Miss Wardell said that the roads were perfect.

So, at nine o'clock, when I went to bed, again I prayed. I don't know how God worked it between nine and ten thirty, but at ten thirty, my father said to me that if the weatherman predicted fair weather, I should call Miss Wardell and tell her to pick me up. So I went to sleep with new hope.

The next day, as soon as I woke up, I got hold of The New York Times and looked at the weather report. A half hour later, I called Miss Wardell and said to her, "Pick me up."

You can guess what the paper said. Isn't God wonderful!!

Arnold was an extremely sincere child in what he was learning about Jesus and the New Testament because of the background of his faith. It all had become real to him. We all found Arnold very extraordinary.

In October of 1957, Arnold wrote in his testimony that God told him what He wanted him to be: "He told me through Luke 24:47, 'And that repentance and remission of sins should be preached in His name, among all nations, beginning at Jerusalem.' I am to become a missionary to the Jews, and I hope to be baptized when I'm eighteen."

Arnold Fruchtenbaum Remembers

Ruth Wardell first came knocking on my family's door in 1957 when I was living on Blake Avenue in the Van Sicklen section of Brooklyn, New York. She came in with a card that had been filled out about six years earlier.

In 1948, three years before we were given visas to come to the U.S., my parents had met a Lutheran Minister and his daughter who visited the Displaced Persons Camp in West Germany where my family was placed after the war ended. This minister would bring clothes and aid for Jewish refugees like my family. He found out that we had applied to emigrate to the U.S. He tore off the cover to a magazine he had and gave it to my mother. It was the October 1948 issue of the Chosen People Ministries magazine. The minister told my mother to contact the people from this organization when we arrived in New York. The address was on the cover that he had torn off. He told her that this organization would help us in our new country. My mother did not know exactly what this organization did. She thought that they merely provided help to new Jewish immigrants to America, which in fact, they did. They also shared the Good News of Jesus Christ. We had no idea that this was what they did.

We arrived in New York in 1951, and my mother went to the address on the magazine cover in Manhattan. She met with Dr. Daniel Fuchs, but due to language differences, all that occurred was that our name and address was written on an index card. This card remained untouched for almost six years.

When Ruth came calling that first time, she spoke to my parents. They hardly understood what she was saying. They were Europeans with language issues that did not allow them to understand much of what Ruth was saying to them. What they thought was that Ruth was from a Jewish group that had something to do with the Bible. When the meeting time for this group came, my parents had no objection to allowing me to attend. My brother, my sister, and I were picked up by car and driven to the meeting where we had our first Bible lesson. This was the first time I had heard about Jesus. The people running the meeting gave each of us a copy of the New Testament. I learned that Chosen People Ministries was a Jewish-Christian group. I thought this was some sort of major contradiction. In my mind, one was either a Jew or a Christian. How could one be both? I concluded that any Jew that believed in Christ had to be suffering from schizophrenia. Since I was having trouble resolving this contradiction, I became angry. Miss Wardell saw my struggle, and rather than trying to reason with me, she challenged me.

My father had trained me well in the Old Testament Scriptures. At the time I met Ruth I was thirteen years old and very interested in Biblical Studies. When Ruth began sharing the Messianic Scriptures from the Old Testament, I challenged all that she said about Jesus having fulfilled those Scriptures. Ruth was working with Eleanor Bullock, Ken Anderson, and Molly Fetner (a young trainee). These people had a different attitude about God than anyone I had ever met before. They talked about God as if they really knew him. The other thing that got my attention was the good teaching Ruth and the others offered on Old Testament prophecy, such as Isaiah 53 and other Messianic Scriptures. The second time I came to class, Ruth showed these to me in the Leeser Bible Translation. Leeser was the

Orthodox Jewish Translation of the Hebrew Bible into English. This was difficult for me to ignore, coming from a translation by a rabbi. Shortly thereafter, I became a believer in Yeshua, Jesus. Ruth kept the Leeser Bible for decades and recently gave it to me. I have put it in my library.

I then became involved in the mission's young adult group, Teens for the Messiah, which later became the Messianic Youth Fellowship. Three times we went off for a weekend to the Liebenzell Center in Hackettstown, New Jersey. My whole life was centered on those retreats. I lived in a *very* Jewish neighborhood with mostly Orthodox Jews. These retreats were the only real contact I had with other Jewish believers. My closest friend lived over one mile away. So, I lived for these fellowships. Even at the East New York center, there were almost no people my age. Even my siblings no longer attended. Meeting Jewish believers who were my

Arnold's Baptism by Dr. Fuchs

age meant a lot to me. These retreats were scheduled many months apart, so I looked forward to them.

In 1958, my family moved to California. Over time, I became like a son to Ruth, and she even gave me a key to her house in Levittown so that whenever I was in New York I had a place to stay even if Ruth was out of town. Even though I was living in California, my heart was with the Messianic Youth Fellowship.

Arnold's Baptism and His Adventures While Witnessing

Ruth Remembers

When Arnold graduated from high school, he left home in California to come to New York to go to school. He was attending Shelton College in Ringwood, New Jersey, which is about an hour from New York City.

One of the first things he wanted to do was to be baptized. This was important to Arnold because his father would not allow him to be baptized as long as Arnold was living at home. In one of his articles, written in October of 1957, Arnold described how God called him to be a missionary to the Jews and that he hoped to be baptized at the age of eighteen. The time had finally come. In 1962, Arnold and some of his friends were baptized by Dr. Daniel Fuchs, Director of Chosen People Ministries. It was a really joyous occasion, and I was thrilled to see Arnold able to fulfill his desires to follow the Lord.

The members of the Messianic Youth Fellowship went out with me almost every other week to speak in churches in New York, New Jersey, Pennsylvania, etc. Arnold, who quite often had to walk three miles to get back to his dorm at Shelton College in Ringwood, never once missed one of those meetings. I remember one time we were in one part of New Jersey, and Arnold was in another part. I thought to myself, "Well, this is one time Arnold won't get here, and he won't get to speak in this church." Suddenly, just before the meeting was about to start, Arnold walked in the church's front door. He had hitch-hiked across New Jersey to get to the meeting.

Baptism Class: Arnold and Friends

It meant a great deal to him to speak at those meetings. He would do whatever it took to attend. What he really enjoyed was the fact that he was with his Jewish friends. What attracted these Jewish people then and still does today is being together with other Jewish believers. There was no monetary compensation for what these young people did. In fact, they paid their own way and even had to buy their own meals. They desired to be together, and they wanted to share their testimonies with people in the church because they were excited about Jesus.

Arnold Continues

Ruth scheduled the group to go to churches where the young people would give their testimonies about how they came to faith. When I was attending Shelton College in Ringwood, just northwest of New York City, Ruth would give me the address of the church where the group was scheduled to speak, and I would make my way there by myself. After the meeting, Ruth would drop me at a train station in New York City, and I would travel to a bus that would leave me in the vicinity of my Shelton College dormitory. If we were late

coming back from the church, the buses would no longer be running. The bus station was three miles from the school, and I would have to walk back to my dormitory. When this happened during the winter, I would sometimes walk the three miles through wind and snow. On occasion, I would get back to my dorm and fall into bed fully dressed. I had to be up at six or seven the next morning, so I just slept in my clothes, got up the next morning, and went to class. This went on for two years as I tried not to miss any meetings of the Messianic Youth Fellowship. When Shelton College moved to Cape May, New Jersey, I did not do much with the Fellowship anymore. From that point on, I always kept in contact but had no direct involvement with the group.

In 1972, Ruth brought a youth group with fifteen people over to Israel where I was living, and I showed them around Israel for one month.

Ruth Remembers

This was my second visit to Israel. We all slept in tents. In the evening, we played and sang Israeli songs. The people would gather around, and Arnold, who spoke Hebrew, would share with them about who we were and what we believed. We all had a very wonderful and informative time in Israel.

God Is Always On Time

It is always amazing to look back and see how God developed His plans for people's lives. After six years, the card with the Fruchtenbaum family information was still in the office of Chosen People Ministries. Arnold and his family were still living at that address. Additionally, the building that the mission rented for the meetings Arnold attended was only available to the ministry for that year. It was during that particular period of time that Arnold attended and accepted the Lord. At the end of that year, we no longer had that building and would probably not have attempted to contact the Fruchtenbaum family. However, God's plans always come to pass. It is a joy to me that God directed my path to be at the right place, at the right time, to be part of the Lord's plan for Arnold's life when he was young.

Arnold has always been kind to me down through these many years. Whenever he came to teach near where I was living, he always called me up and took me out for dinner. I have attended Camp Shoshanah several times, and I have been greatly blessed by his teaching.

I am very proud of all the accomplishments of my son in the faith, Arnold.

Camp Shoshanah

Camp Shoshanah is nestled in the Adirondack Mountains in northern New York, about one hour south of Montreal. When Arnold was a teenager, he qualified for this camp by memorizing many Scripture verses. As a result, he went to this camp for many summers. The camp was run by Burl Haynie, who became a close friend and mentor to Arnold.

This camp has become a focal point in Arnold's life. He met his wife, Mary Ann, at camp. Years later, his ministry was given ownership of the campgrounds. Every summer, for over thirty years, Camp Shoshanah draws people from all over the world to study with fine teachers who teach the Bible from a Jewish perspective.

Mary Ann Fruchtenbaum, Wife of Arnold Fruchtenbaum, Remembers

Arnold and Mary Ann Fruchtenbaum

When I met Arnold, he was a young teenager. I knew that he had become a believer and that Ruth was his spiritual "Mom." I met her many years later at a CPM Summer's End Conference, about one year before Arnold and I were married. I knew that Arnold had been given the key to her house and that Ruth was a part of the family that had replaced his own. It was important for me to get to know Ruth. Arnold and I became engaged to be married. We were planning to get married at the Chosen People Ministries building on 72nd Street in New York. The planning for the wedding was helped along by "Mom" Wardell. We had arranged for Dr. Daniel Fuchs to preside over the marriage ceremony.

I spent the entire week leading up to the wedding at Mom Wardell's house, and it was a blessing because, from there, Ruth was able to assist with the many arrangements that needed to be finalized, especially for the reception. Having spent those days working closely with Ruth, I was impressed by the way she included God in every aspect of her day. What I remember most is that Ruth told me that when she wakes up in the morning, she thanks God for another day and then asks Him what it is that He wants her to do that day. This helped me to deal with those days that were not going well because of circumstances or people. I remembered how Ruth would start her day, and I would just ask God what I should do in those difficult situations. In the long run, this lesson that I learned from Ruth was lifesaving. I discovered that working in Jewish missions was not only harder than other missions, but that it was probably ten times as hard. Learning to speak to God on a regular basis throughout the day helped me to get through the toughest of days. This was all thanks to Ruth's model.

In Jewish ministry, if you do not have a thick skin, you will not be successful. A lot of people coming out of a Gentile Christian culture are confused about how to deal with Jewish people who are straightforward. Ruth had the capacity and the personality to know that understanding this would be a requirement. Ruth modeled for me how to respond so that when working with Jewish people, I would not take offense at certain statements they might make. So, when Jewish women would refer to me as a *schiksa* (Yiddish for a Gentile woman—with a mild negative connotation), I never took it as a negative comment. I would smile and say something like, "Yes, I am." I learned from Ruth that the important thing was whether or not they listened when you taught. Their comments were not important in comparison to sharing the Gospel with them. No matter what people said or how they tried to divert from the lesson, the missionary's job was to bring them back to the Gospel message.

Year after year, our relationship grew closer. I always feel so much love from Ruth. When the congregation held an eightieth birthday party for her, Arnold and I went to Dallas to share this event with her and to encourage her. We encourage each other whenever possible, whether it is by phone or e-mail, etc. It has been exciting to know Ruth all of these years.

Ruth's Commentary

The party for my eightieth birthday was a great joy to me, and I was especially blessed that Arnold and Mary Ann took the time out of their busy schedule to spend this time with me.

CHAPTER 8
New Missions: Queens, Far Rockaway, Huntington Station, Lindenhurst, and Levittown, NY

In 1954, besides the mission station that we established in East New York where Arnold came to meetings, we also were able to establish missions in Queens, Far Rockaway, Huntington Station, Lindenhurst, and Levittown, New York. The reason that these different missions started all at the same time was that many of the people who were attending the different events taking place at the Brooklyn Mission were moving out to Long Island. In addition, the Jewish population was shifting from Brooklyn to Long Island. This was a time when people were becoming more mobile as a result of cheaper automobiles, and many in New York City were moving to suburban towns where they could own their own homes. Levittown was a community where they built track housing, which was affordable and attractive to people looking to escape New York City. I lived there for fifteen years.

I worked with a team, which I felt was far better than working alone at a particular station. Teams are much better since you can have one person dedicated to the men's ministry, another to the women's ministry, and yet another to the children's ministry, which consisted of all age groups of children. I was trained for working with children, so that became my part of the work. This team approach placed the best people in the best places for them, and they were thereby very effective. We had a good team, and many people came to faith as a result of the branches on Long Island, Queens, Huntington Station, Far Rockaway, Lindenhurst, and Levittown.

At first, the meetings in Levittown were held in my home. I fixed up the garage as a place for the children and teens to play and do handicrafts. We had singing, prayer, and Bible study in the living room. Then the mission rented a house where we conducted our women's meetings, children's meetings, etc. We had the great joy of seeing many Jewish people come to faith in Jesus.

Once each month, all five stations on Long Island would meet together in Westbury, New York. We had special speakers at these times. Some would be Messianic believers who would share their testimonies. These meetings were well-attended and enjoyable. This is also the place where we would have the Christmas program and an Easter celebration (we called it Resurrection Day)—where we would teach the Messianic prophecies about the death and resurrection of the Messiah. This period of time was from 1957 to 1967.

Sally Fradkin

Sally Fradkin became a Jewish believer before we had met her. She had contacted the New York City mission station of Chosen People Ministries, and they had given her my name because I did not live too far from her on Long Island. Sally had become a believer, but her husband had not. However, Sally's husband did allow her to have her belief, and he did welcome us into their home. Before the mission actually had a place to meet in Levittown, we were meeting in Sally Fradkin's home.

When I visited Sally's home, I would bring along another mission worker, Mrs. Beatrice Maggi. We would have a Bible study together. Sally had a great thirst for the Word of God. Eventually, she became great friends with Bea Maggi. That was the beginning of our work in Levittown, Long Island. Then the mission rented a home in Levittown, and shortly thereafter we started children's classes there. When we started women's classes, Sally would come to the meetings every week.

In the following anecdotes, Sally tells how God worked in her life and how she became a believer. She also relates how, after forty-five years of faithful prayer, her husband also accepted his Messiah. Wow!

Sally Fradkin Remembers

As I stood on the roof of our New York City apartment building, I wondered if a six-story fall would kill me. Since I didn't know the answer, I decided not to jump. The decision changed nothing. I went downstairs to the quiet rooms below. My husband was out looking for work, and my parents were caring for my little girl while I recuperated from a recent miscarriage.

In time, my body recovered, but the grief and anger of losing a child continued. When I went to get my daughter, my mother sensed that something was very wrong. She then did a strange thing for an Orthodox Jewish woman to do. She handed me a book entitled, *The Greatest Story Ever Told.* "Here. Your brother has been reading this. Maybe it will help," she said.

My daughter and I returned to our apartment, and after tucking her into bed, I opened the book. I read about a Jewish carpenter named Joseph and his pregnant wife Mary. To comply with Caesar's census, they made a trip to the city of Bethlehem. The book asked the question, "What do Romans care about Jewish wives and their babies?"

The thought struck me—Mary was a Jewish wife. She too had been pregnant, but she gave birth to a living child, a very special child. Having read fragments of the New Testament, I considered myself to be very tolerant. I agreed that Jesus was a great teacher in Israel, but the Son of God? Never! The idea went against everything that I'd ever been taught.

Still, the book fascinated me. My husband worked nights now, and once my daughter was asleep, I'd turn to it. I didn't just read the book—I devoured it. In it, author Fulton Oursler, paralleled the four gospels.

I soon learned that Jesus never claimed to be a great teacher. He said that He was the Messiah of Israel, the One promised to my people. I decided He must either be suffering from delusions, or He was who He claimed to be. As I read the accounts of His miracles, I was struck by His compassion for the Jewish people. This was not a carved figure holding out hands in a church. This was a living, breathing man.

Gradually, my ideas began to change. By the time I read His prayer in the Garden of Gethsemane, I knew He was the promised Son of God and my Messiah. In Matthew 26:39, Jesus/Yeshua said, "My Father, if it be possible, may this cup be taken from Me. Yet not as I will, but as You will." Something inside compelled me to repeat His words. It was the first honest prayer I'd ever spoken.

I knew little about salvation, and even less about confession of sins, but my life had changed. The day-to-day struggle continued. I still had to chase after an active toddler and stretch a meager income to put food on our table, but now I had new strength. The depression had lifted.

The idea of walking into a church was unthinkable. I was an Orthodox Jew who somehow had come to believe that Jesus was the Messiah. In itself, that fact made me wonder if I had lost my mind.

Sally, Bea Maggi, Bea's daughter, Ruth, and Sally's children

To find the answers that I so desperately needed, I bought a pocket edition of the Bible and began to read the New Testament. I soon finished the four gospels—no easy task with a young child running around the house. About the time I started to read the Old Testament, I turned on the black-and-white television that we had bought in better days. The year was 1951, and I heard this television evangelist speaking about the love of God and the plan of salvation that had existed since the beginning of time. Those words went from my head to my heart, and I realized that God was going to hold me to the commitment that I had made when I had spoken those words from Matthew 26:39, "Yet not as I will, but as You will." Just as Jesus had confessed, I realized that I now also had surrendered my will to the Father.

Soon thereafter, I learned that I was not the only Jew to believe in Jesus. There was a mission to the Jews, not far from my home. Gearing up my courage, I took the subway to ABMJ. As I hesitantly entered the door to the mission, a gray-haired man greeted me. I was full of questions since I did not know what to expect. My first question wasn't how I could serve the Lord. The first thing I asked this man was, "Can I still keep a kosher home?" In typical Jewish style, he answered my question with a question. He said, "What's wrong with kosher meat?"

In answer to a request for information, the mission sent Ruth Wardell and another woman (Bea Maggi) to my home. They came to study the Bible with me. I remember that Ruth taught from the Book of Daniel, and I was completely baffled by the prophetic meaning of the golden-headed statue.

Shortly thereafter, the mission opened a study group in a Levittown house. As far as I knew, it was the first mission outreach on Long Island. Ruth was one of the many missionaries who taught there. She also watched the children while other missionaries taught. This was no small task because my four-year-old son was a hyperactive child. Our class was composed of both Jewish and Gentile unbelieving women.

As time passed, I did learn from the mission teachers how to serve Jesus/Yeshua and how to live the new life He'd given me. I began by telling my husband that Yeshua was now my Messiah. In the 1950s, Jews who followed Jesus were usually thrown out of the house. I expected it would happen to me. Instead, my husband was quiet for a moment, and then said, "I love you. Stay with me. We will work things out."

Working things out produced some strange results. For one thing, we had a very confused mailman. *The Synagogue Light*, an Orthodox Jewish publication, usually arrived in our mailbox on the same day as the Christian magazine, *Decision*.

For me, it was the beginning of a long walk with my Messiah, Yeshua. Back then we called Him Jesus. I made many friends along the way and learned much about the Bible and Jesus from my friend Ruth Wardell.

The Story of Sally Fradkin's Husband's Coming to Faith

In his Sabbath message, our Congregational Leader told us that as believers in Yeshua (Jesus), we were the Bride of the Messiah. By using ancient Jewish wedding customs, he compared the bridegroom's coming to claim his bride with the Lord's return for His people.

Sally Fradkin and Husband

The leader sang a song that he said the Lord had given to him, the *Song of the Bridegroom*. Our Messianic Congregation responded with the *Song of the Bride*. As we lifted our voices to our heavenly Bridegroom, I had the mental image of taking my husband's hand and leading him under the wedding canopy. My husband was not yet a believer.

I recalled a time just a few months before, when the leader taught a similar message. At that time, some of the men of the congregation erected a traditional wedding canopy, called a *Chuppa*. The leader called the entire congregation forward to stand under the canopy. As believers, this was symbolic of us as the church awaiting our Bridegroom, Jesus. I turned to my husband and asked my husband to accept Yeshua and come forward with me. As he had done for the previous forty-five years, he shook his head no and once again refused. With tears in my eyes, I went forward and stood under the canopy alone.

A sister in the Lord tried to comfort me and said, "Maybe he'll come next time."

"Maybe never," I replied.

After forty-five years, I didn't think that my prayers for my husband's salvation would ever be answered. I had tried to claim the promise of Acts 16:31, "Believe in the Lord Jesus, and you will be saved—you and your household."

We had finished singing the *Song of the Bride.* As I stood there praying for healing mercies, I was suddenly aware of someone taking my hand. I looked up and there was my husband by my side, smiling and nodding that he was ready to accept Jesus as his Messiah.

The men of the congregation immediately gathered around my husband as the leader led him in the prayer that not only brought him into God's kingdom but also made our household one in the Lord. After forty-five years, my prayers had been answered! I wish that I could say that over all of those long years I'd been faithful in my prayers, but the truth is that our marriage barely survived. Through everything, God provided for me not only physically, but mentally and spiritually as well.

At services, we used to share my Bible whenever the leader referred to a verse of Scripture. However, now my husband has his own Bible, which he has already begun to mark with many reference tabs. As I look at the tabs, I think that each one is a reminder that with God, nothing is impossible. Without being aware, my prayer had been answered immediately. It just took forty-five years to travel from God's throne to my husband's heart.

Clara Rubin

Clara Rubin was one of the believing Jewish workers out on Long Island. Clara has worked for the mission most of her life, predominantly as a volunteer. She worked with Eleanor Bullock, Jo and Bill Ennis, and me. Clara's history with ABMJ goes back to when she was a teenager in 1928. She knew Miss Sussdorf, who had worked for the ministry in the early 1900s. Clara was a very evangelistic type of person who had no fear in witnessing to everyone.

She would witness anywhere, at any time, to any group or individual, and was also very helpful with the children's ministries. We used to have our youth meetings in her house. She opened her home for us to have meetings in a special room that she had reserved for us. Her goal was that she wanted to see Jewish people like herself come to know Jesus. I worked alongside her with the children. Clara and her husband Joe had a daughter, Ilayna, who was one of my students.

Clara's mother was not a believer, and she did not want to hear about Jesus, even if one called him by his Hebrew name, Yeshua. She was raised in Orthodox Judaism, and she did not want to hear that name. She said it would break her heart if her granddaughter Ilayna married a Gentile. When a young man came to call on Ilayna, Clara would ask him "Are you Jewish?" and she would also ask him if he was a believer. If he was not interested in learning the Scriptures, he need not come again. This frustration and stress happened so many times that it led to Clara's mother going to the hospital.

Clara's sisters called saying, "You are killing Mama," but Clara was determined and prayed that Ilayna would marry a Jewish believer who was a college graduate and had parents involved in Jewish mission work. Ilayna's grandmother said to her daughter, "Clara, if such a boy ever comes along, and my granddaughter ever gets married, that's the day I will become a believer in Jesus."

David Klayman, Ilayna Klayman, and Clara Rubin

Jewish people need a sign. The sign that this grandmother needed came about when Ilayna met David Klayman at a Hebrew Christian Alliance banquet in New York City. David was a Hebrew Christian and attended college on Long Island, where he lived with his parents. As Jewish believers who had also experienced many years of separation from their families after they came to faith in Jesus, they were active in ministries that reached out to Jew and Gentile alike.

The year 1963 was a most eventful one. David graduated, completed active military reserve training, and married Ilayna. Then her grandmother said, "If the Messiah could do this, then He has to be true." Clara knew that this was the only way for her mother to become a believer. She had been witnessed to so many times, but this was the sign that she needed, and she became a believer in Yeshua.

David and Ilayna had two sons, Mark and Joel, and they also had Ruth Wardell as their teacher in the mission. They attended the mission summer camp and took part in many of Ruth's youth activities. Ilayna's grandmother lived to see her two great-grandsons celebrate their thirteenth birthdays where they read from the Bible, both from the Old and the New Testaments and spoke of how they had also come to faith in Jesus.

Now, forty-five years later, Clara not only has a daughter and son-in-law who love the Lord, but two grandsons and their wives, and four great-granddaughters who are being brought up in homes which all love Jesus.

Clara Rubin Recalls (at Age Ninety-Two)

I have been involved with the ABMJ, now known as Chosen People Ministries, since 1917. I had the pleasure of knowing Ruth Wardell since the first day that she came to ABMJ from Canada more than sixty years ago. God gifted her with a talent for children from kindergarteners to teens. She worked in Brooklyn and Hollis, Queens. She started the Levittown branch, as well as helped me with my children's classes in Huntington Station, Long Island. The children all loved her. She would take the teens to speak in churches and always took them to places of interest that they would enjoy. Miss Wardell led many children to Jesus, and a good number of them are in God's service today. Some are even working with Chosen People Ministries.

The thing that I remember most about working for the mission was that for us there was no such thing as hours or days. Ruth and others worked night and day to get the job done.

Young People from the Brooklyn Mission

Sandra (Sandy) Schoenblum

Sandy Schoenblum and Arnold Fruchtenbaum

Sandy Schoenblum came from the old Brooklyn Seigel Street area. Seigel Street is an area of Brooklyn where many Orthodox Jewish people lived. Several Jewish families living in this neighborhood attended functions that we held at the mission. It was there that Sandy came to know the Lord. Her mother and father did not become believers, and they opposed Sandy's choice to accept Jesus as her Messiah. Most parents did not come to faith, but many were impressed by the things that their children were learning at the mission, and they saw positive attributes being developed in their children. On the other hand, some parents did come to faith as a result of what their children shared about the Jewish Messiah, Jesus.

For many of the children from this neighborhood, the mission was one of the few places they felt comfortable and accepted. Sandy was a great student of the Word of God, and she knew who she was as a Jewish person believing in Jesus. She was very strong in her faith and was a great *kibbitzer* (talker) who loved to laugh. Sandy loved to go speaking in churches.

She eventually became one of our teachers with the children at the mission in Queens. Sandy and a friend, Sonia, would come to the mission every Friday night faithfully to teach the children the Word of God. She also helped with the outings and camp. It is sad that she died so young in her mid-forties, but that was God's time for her to enter Heaven. Everybody who met Sandra loved her. She had a special place in people's hearts.

Sandy Schoenblum's Testimony

I was born into a Conservative Jewish home in the Williamsburg section of Brooklyn. Both of my parents were raised in Orthodox

Jewish homes but did not attend synagogue regularly except on the high holy days. When I was about four or five years old, my mother took me to the Brooklyn Branch of the American Board of Missions to the Jews which was located two blocks from our home. My mother was afraid to let her father, an Orthodox Jew from Russia, know that she attended the mission. My grandfather was forced to flee from Russia in the early 1900s because of religious persecution, and so it is quite obvious that he despised any religious group that involved Christianity. For many years, my grandfather would not walk on the same block where a church was located. My aunts and uncles all attended Hebrew School, and my uncles were all Bar Mitzvahed in the synagogue having been taught to fear people of other religious convictions. My mother attended the mission whenever my grandfather was away from his business so that he would not get upset. My mother always referred to the mission as the "club" so that her Jewish friends would not persecute her.

I also grew up fearing to accept Christ before my friends because of religious persecution. I could not endure their saying that I was no longer a Jew because I had accepted Christ. I had a quiet witness for the Lord for many years.

I first went to camp when I was seven years old, and it was then that I accepted Christ as my Savior. I was not sure what this meant, but I knew I wanted Him in my life. God really showed me that He was a reality in my life when I was saved from drowning. I knew then that I was spared for a reason.

During my early teens I grew away from the Lord, primarily because I stopped going to the mission and lacked Christian fellowship. The summer that I was thirteen, I was given another opportunity to attend camp. It was during this camp program that I accepted the fact that Christ truly died for my sins and that He wanted my life for His service. This was the turning point in my young life. It was the conviction that I had a personal Lord and Savior that saw me through persecution from my relatives, family, and friends.

I attended a secular college in Manhattan where the Lord provided wonderful and faithful Christian friends through Inter-Varsity

Christian Fellowship. This, in addition to the mission, provided an excellent growing experience for me in the Christian faith. No longer did I fear telling people that I was a Christian. When I was nineteen, I accepted the challenge of being baptized in our mission. It was a big step for me, as my parents did not approve. Nevertheless, I felt that it was really God's will for my life to step forward for Him. My parents threatened not to come to the baptism which caused me great consternation and sadness. But, I prayed that they would come if they really loved me and respected my decision. God answered my prayer, and they came to the mission, took an active part in the hymn singing, and gave me their blessings. I could not contain my joy.

Since then, I have put my hope and trust in Jesus Christ and have tried to live for Him. It has not been easy as we are still in a mortal body. I also wish that I could give young people a simple formula for Christian growth, but since our Lord is a personal God, He reaches into each person's heart and deals with it. Since I have let the Lord lead my life, I have found an inner peace that surpasses any earthly comprehension.

Lou and Sonia Viegas

Sonia and Lou Viegas

Sonia attended the mission in Brooklyn. I had taken on the responsibility of the children's ministries in the Old Williamsburg Mission and worked with those children for quite a while in the 1950s. I've known Sonia since she was a very young girl of nine or ten years old. She came to the Old Williamsburg Mission. She lived nearby with her mother and four sisters. I became acquainted with all five of them. They attended our summer camp program. When she became a teenager, she joined us at the Messianic Youth Fellowship. On Friday nights, we would go to the Old Brooklyn Mission and have big meetings there with the young people from many different mission stations. They had fabulous times. They loved to pray together and to fellowship. They also loved to study the Bible. We had these big Friday night youth groups in which Sonia was very much involved. Her sisters Pauline and Loretta also came. She met her husband Lou at one of these meetings. They married and became involved with our summer camp program as counselors and worked at camp for a few summers.

Sonia was and still is always joyful in the Lord. In speaking with her recently, she shared how she is rejoicing at what the Lord has done in her whole life. They were a wonderful couple in that they took a girl into their home who never advanced beyond the abilities of a three-year-old. They loved and cared for her for thirty years. This girl required a lot of care, so they had to send her to a home that could better care for her needs. However, they still have close contact and every Sunday, they go pick her up and she spends the day with them.

Lou and Sonia never had any children of their own. They also took care of other young people in their home. One of the other young girls who came to live with them did not have parents, so Lou and Sonia became like parents to her. She married a Jewish fellow, and they had two children. Lou and Sonia adopted them as grandchildren, and they have become an integral part of that family. Grandparenting has become very exciting for them. The children come frequently to stay at Grandma and Grandpa's house on Long Island, New York.

Lou and Sonia have honored the Lord in everything that they have done.

Without the mission, Sonia would not have become what she is today. I'm still in contact with her, and I am pleased that her mind and heart are still very much set on the Lord.

Sonia (Storey) Viegas Remembers

I was four years old when I was introduced to ABMJ by my Jewish grandmother and mom, who attended women's Bible study and sewing class in Williamsburg, Brooklyn. When I turned eleven years old, Ruth Wardell came into my life when she came to Brooklyn to start a young teen's Bible study. Ruth had been working with youngsters on Long Island for some time, but now she came to tackle the kids from Williamsburg. She turned out to be a wonderful, loving, and happy person who really showed she cared for us. She taught us that it was possible to learn to love the Lord as our Messiah and to grow in His love and still have lots of fun and be happy as believers in the process! There was no room for sour faces in our group because our Lord is a loving and happy Lord.

Ruth started a Friday night Bible study. She played piano, and most of the time we would just keep singing hymns. We always had prayer time. Our faith was strengthened with Ruth's guidance as she taught us the Word of God.

She would often take groups of teens to churches to give our testimonies as to how we came to know Jesus. I would always complain that I just couldn't speak in public! But when the time came, you could not stop me or any of us, and it was because she never gave up on us. She was always encouraging us. These memories are just a small example of why Ruth was the greatest positive influence in my life and why I thank God everyday for her dedication and passion for the Jewish people and young kids like me.

Later on, Ruth had a Bible class for young kids between six and twelve years old. My friend Sandy Schoenblum (who was about sixteen years old at the time) and I would help Ruth. When Ruth couldn't be there, she left Sandy and me in charge. We would have to get all the kids to and from the class. She would leave us some money, and the rest was up to us. We didn't drive, so we had to use the trains. We had to go into some really rough neighborhoods, but we knew the Lord was with us and was our protection. As a result of Ruth's trusting us with this responsibility, we grew into independent young women and were forever grateful for her help in our growth in our faith.

I had the privilege of sharing in the summer camping program. Ruth was in charge of the camp, which was in Pennsylvania. I soon became a JC (Junior Counselor). At the end of a stressful, hard day, she would take us out for a ride. The roads in Pennsylvania were pitch dark at night. All of a sudden, she'd shut off the headlights and all you could see were the glowing eyes of the animals in the surrounding woods. We were scared to death and screaming. However, our screams of fright would soon turn to gales of laughter. The stresses of the day were gone!

Sonia Tells of A Trip To Ruth's Bible School

Each and every trip I took with Ruth was eventful, and this one was no exception! This trip included Mrs. Wardell (Ruth's mom), my best friend Sandy Schoenblum, Gloria (a fellow student from Northeastern), and me. We all piled into the back of Ruth's station wagon and proceeded to take the best trip I ever had. We sang hymns and prayed as we drove along. The whole trip was filled with the joy of the Lord. At one point, Ruth let Gloria drive, and she and I sat in the back with the tailgate down, waving at kids in other cars and laughing and having a grand old time. Ruth's mom, who was a saintly and very prim and proper lady, would say in her prim and proper voice, "Girls, calm down!" This, of course, evoked more silliness from us. All I could think was, "This crazy lady (Ruth) is a missionary! Oh my!" What we learned from Ruth was that we could be believers but still be happy and have wonderful, fun times. Seeing how Ruth lived her life and how happy she was made us desire to know and serve the Lord she so loved.

I am personally blessed for knowing Ruth and having her in my life. It is through her influence and teaching that I wanted the Lord in my life. It was through her guidance that I grew in the Lord. It was through her deep love for the Jewish people that our little group became family. It was through her faithful service that, to this very day, I continue to try to maintain the things she taught me.

Lou Viegas Remembers

I met Ruth through my wife Sonia when we started dating each other. I had heard from the friend who introduced us that Ruth was someone who was "religious and worked for the mission." I was a "lapsed Catholic" and had no idea what this "mission" thing was. I thought about the Bowery Mission that ministered to the homeless and figured what the heck! I remember the first time Sonia brought me to the Brooklyn Mission on a Friday. It was then that I met Ruth Wardell. I affectionately referred to her as "Hurricane Ruth" because she was a constant whirlwind of activity. As I recall, she put me right to work, helping move furniture, speaking with kids, serving refreshments, etc. Man, she was the super delegator of all time!

As I came to know her better, I knew why my future wife loved her so. Her love of God was as evident as the hair on her head. She lived, breathed, and exuded the Spirit. As I got to know her better, I found her way of spreading the Word came from her deep belief and love of God. What a great messenger of the Almighty. Her example made it easier for me to come back into the spiritual fold. I learned about loving God and being a more forgiving person through her. I also learned that she was a super motivator who got things accomplished through others, yet made them think it was their idea!

The summer after we got married, I found myself at Camp Sar Shalom in Pennsylvania with a house full of little ones. I was exhausted and loving every minute. I saw the miracle of children transformed from gritty, nasty city kids to gentle, God-loving souls through her guidance and example—and saw myself being transformed at the same time.

Christmas at the Mission

It was my joy to share Yeshua with Jewish people in New York City as far back as 1946. As a missionary with ABMJ, I recall that some of our greatest times of outreach happened through holiday services. I'm not talking about Rosh Hashanah, Yom Kippur, and others from Leviticus 23. We taught about these holidays in our Bible classes at the mission centers, and the people celebrated them in their homes. However, we did not begin public celebrations of Passover or the Fall Feasts until the '60s. So what did we do before that? We celebrated Christmas and Easter! Christmas was the perfect time to talk about the following Scriptures:

Micah 5:2, "But as for you, Bethlehem Ephrathah, too little to be among the clans of Judah, from you One will go forth for Me to be ruler in Israel. His goings forth are from long ago, from the days of eternity."

Isaiah 7:14, "Therefore the Lord Himself will give you a sign: Behold, a virgin will be with child and bear a son, and she will call His name Immanuel."

Isaiah 9:6, "For a child will be born to us, a son will be given to us; and the government will rest on His shoulders; and His name will be called Wonderful Counselor, Mighty God, Eternal Father, Prince of Peace."

Christmas was our biggest event of the year, and each service would be packed. In the four services, at least 400 to 500 Jewish people attended, and fifty or more were Jewish people who did not yet know Jesus. People not only came, but they enjoyed it—and many found Yeshua as their Messiah. One of the main reasons they came to faith was the strong emphasis on teaching Messianic prophecies concerning the birth of Jesus. We had five programs in Westbury, Long Island, Flushing, Coney Island, Manhattan, and Brooklyn. The way that people were invited to these programs was through invitations from the people who attended the mission. They were given flyers, which they could give to their friends, which would invite them to a Christmas program. This was so well-attended that you could not get another person into that room. The old Williamsburg Mission was also filled with people. This was still going on, even in the 1940s, '50s, and '60s. You couldn't have gotten a bigger crowd even if you had gone out and advertised these meetings. There just was no room to put any more people.

I recall many Christmas programs at the mission. I dressed all the children as shepherds and sheep. One time when I went to Israel, I took two slide pictures of the shepherd's field near Bethlehem. When the slides were projected on the screen and put side by side we would have a panoramic view. Then I put the children, who were dressed as shepherds and sheep, in front of the projection so that they would look like they were in the shepherd's field in Bethlehem. It was special.

These services also made a lasting impression on the children who performed the dramatic plays. Recently, I was chatting with a woman who remembered her part in one such play. She said, "It was very important, when I was growing up as a Jewish child, to know that Christmas was a Jewish holiday. After all, Mary, Joseph, and the shepherds were all Jewish, and this was very exciting to me. I remember very well the parts that referred to Messianic prophecies and how thrilled I was to know that they were fulfilled in Jesus. I loved the carols we sang, and I was especially blessed with 'O Come, O Come Emmanuel.' It was my favorite, and even to this day (some forty years later), I cannot sing it without tears in

my eyes because it means so much to me. The chorus was great: 'Rejoice! Rejoice! Emmanuel shall come to thee, O Israel.' I was greatly impressed with the large crowds of Jewish people who came. Many were not believers, like my Jewish neighbor, a Holocaust survivor, and her two children. It was a great blessing to me to celebrate Christmas and to know it was a Jewish holiday."

Let's give Jewish children the privilege of enjoying Christmas, their best holiday in the whole world.

As I reflect on these activities, I find it interesting that so many Jewish people came to these Christian celebrations. Of course, the mission would teach Christmas and Easter as actually being Jewish holidays since Jesus is the Jewish heart of Christianity. The children were really excited to learn that Christmas was a Jewish holiday because now they could participate in this holiday rather than just being observers. This was marvelous for the Jewish children, but unfortunately, I believe that we have lost that element in the Messianic Congregations. The biggest Jewish holiday in the whole world is the holiday of Christmas because it celebrates the coming of the Jewish Messiah to the earth. Messiah's birth is the culmination of everything. I am amazed that some Messianic Congregations will not even talk about this. The shepherds were Jewish. Joseph was Jewish. Mary was Jewish. All the people involved in the birth of Christ were Jewish. No one should avoid the Jewishness of this beautiful celebration.

When I first started working at the Jewish missions, I was very excited to share the Christmas story with Jewish people. If I told the story correctly, these Jewish people would open up and realize and accept the fact that Christmas is indeed a Jewish holiday. I still tell people that Christmas is the greatest holiday in the whole world, and it's Jewish because on this day we celebrate the birth of the Jewish Messiah. Everyone in the Christmas story is Jewish. How could it not be a Jewish holiday?

CHAPTER 9
Summer Camp

Camp Hananeel, 1949

We had a large number of children in all of our branches in New York, and many went to camp with us every summer. It was at these camps that many children came to know Jesus. The first camp I was involved with was on Long Island near Stony Brook, New York. The name of the camp was Camp Hananeel. This was an established camp that the mission would rent for one month. The mission was there for the first three years that I was with them, from 1947–1950. The children who attended the classes at the mission on a regular basis during the year could attend without any cost to the family.

When we were in the planning stages for the camp, Joseph Hoffman Cohn told me that if I did not run the camp that summer then they would not have a camp that year. Since I had run camp programs before I came to the mission, I saw no reason to cancel camp for that summer, and I accepted the challenge of heading up the camp program. I started with ABMJ in October of 1946, and three months later I was asked to head up the camp. We divided the month into two sessions, each lasting twelve days. The first group consisted of children who were seven to twelve years old. We would use the weekend between sessions to prepare for the next group which was made up of the older teens who stayed the final two weeks. Camping programs at Stony Brook were good. There were always eighty or ninety Jewish children in attendance. Occasionally 100 would attend.

Jeannie Lockerbie Stephenson

Jeannie Lockerbie is the daughter of my friend Jeanette Lockerbie. When Jeannie was a young teen, she worked at the summer camp. She was one of our first counselors. She studied to be a nurse and then prepared to become a missionary to Bangladesh. She was a marvelous missionary there. Now Jeannie and her husband go to Bangladesh to do seminars for the people. They are well-known in that area of the world, and they have been written up in many magazines.

Jeannie Lockerbie Stephenson Remembers

"God is Gracious"

Jeannie Lockerbie Stephenson

My first job, my first train ride, my first near-death situation—all of these revolve around Ruth Wardell. Ruth was a young missionary with ABMJ. Part of her time was spent working in Brooklyn. In 1951, the Lockerbie family also moved to Brooklyn where my dad became pastor of Bay Ridge Baptist Church. I don't recall how we met Ruth, but it was natural. Her father, Glen Wardell, and mine, E.A. Lockerbie, were pastors in a group later called the Fellowship of Evangelical Baptists in Canada.

Our first summer in Brooklyn, Ruth organized a camp for Jewish children. She recruited three young people from Bay Ridge Baptist to help. The three of us—Stuart, Marie, and I—were on what today would be called a "missions trip." We didn't know that term back then. With a group of boys and girls not much younger than we were, we boarded the Long Island Railroad for a fifty-mile journey from Brooklyn to Stony Brook. Ruth assigned me a job as one of the dishwashers. Washing dishes was nothing new, but Ruth had to explain kosher laws. Kosher means "clean." She had promised the children's parents that the food, the preparation, and cleaning up would strictly follow Jewish dietary laws. So I learned to wash dishes used for dairy products in one tub, then change to another tub for a different set of dishes used for meat products. This is because the Jewish kosher laws do not permit the eating of meat with milk products.

Another job that I was given was to corral the kids when we took them on walks around the campus and down to the town's beach on the rocky shore of Long Island Sound. That part of Long Island Sound was known for a wicked undertow, and we were careful to keep the kids close to the shore. So, I have no idea how it was that I got out into the current, and as a novice swimmer, was soon in over my head literally and figuratively. Stuart noticed my situation and signaled to boats at the adjacent yacht club who came to my rescue. All three of those Bay Ridge young people grew up to serve the Lord. Stuart became a pastor, Marie a pastor's wife, and I a missionary in Bangladesh.

The camp was called Hananeel, the meaning of which was reflected in the first lines of the camp's song:

"Hananeel in Hebrew means

God is gracious, don't you see..."

God was gracious to me that summer, sparing my life, and allowing me to learn from one of His gracious servants, Ruth Wardell.

Joys of Summer Camp

A lot of children came to faith in the Lord at our summer camp. I called this the "reaping ground." The reason for this was that the child was immersed in the activities of the mission for ten days. I say that it took three days to get the "world" out of the child and then a few more days to get the "Word" into the child. The children were told to leave the comic books at home, and we did not allow radios either. If we did allow these items, the world would creep into the camp and prevent the Word from getting into the child. We had at least three hours of worship time each day. The children would sing hymns, worship, memorize Scriptures, etc., and they would enjoy it.

A typical day at camp would be something like this. We would wake up in the morning and have devotions with the children in their groups. Then breakfast was served. After that we would attend chapel for at least one hour and fifteen minutes. Next, the children would play some games and by then it was time for lunch. This was followed by an hour of rest. The afternoon was a time for swimming. The walk to the swimming area on Long Island Sound was over one mile. There was a long pier that went out into the water and it was alongside this pier that we used to swim. The water currents were quite strong in Long Island Sound, so we had to be very observant or someone could be caught up in the current and dragged out to sea and possibly drowned. On our last summer there, we almost lost a child in the strong current, and as a result, the mission decided to change the camp location and we did not renew our time at Stony Brook.

Our next camp was Camp Tel Hai in the Lancaster area of Pennsylvania in the Amish country. Emily (Lichtenstein) Seemar, her brother, and her sister attended the mission meetings in Levittown, New York. She was saved as a child at Camp Tel Hai. Many years later, when she was fifty years old, she got to stay at this camp overnight and give her testimony to the people who ran the camp. Emily was thrilled to be there, and they were thrilled to have her there.

Camp Reunion at Camp Tel Hai 2009

Emily's Testimony

This is Emily's testimony about her camp experience which she wrote for *"Ha-Adouth – The Witness"* (Nov. – Dec. 1971), the monthly newsletter for the Messianic Youth Fellowship (MYF). MYF was the youth group that I led in Hollis, New York.

> The moment I set foot onto the camp bus, way back when I was twelve years old, it was to me as if I was setting foot into a total new area and experience in my life. I was actually on a bus heading toward the mission camp. It was my first time out of New York and my first time out in the country. A dream come true is the only way I can describe it!
>
> You see, it had been a long, hard struggle for my brother, sister, and me to finally get permission from my father, allowing us to go. For years, we felt my mother's enthusiasm to bring us to the mission and

my father's definite disapproval. But, finally, that moment we had been waiting for arrived, and he said, "OK," though very skeptically.

So I found myself in the middle of a camp, with many kids like myself. The atmosphere was beautiful, and the realization that this was God's creation, even at the age of twelve, was found in my heart. I knew I loved this place and knew God wanted me there for a reason. Those Gentile missionaries had something that I wanted. They were giving up their lives to tell me about Someone, and I wanted that Someone! So, one night in camp, I can remember my sister and me sitting next to each other, enjoying the usual meeting with Mr. Ennis. He then gave an invitation, and we both knew that we had to go forward. We were scared to death, but together we raised our hands, went out with Betty Smith and Shirley Silver, and accepted the Lord! This is the most vivid thing in my mind about Camp Sar Shalom—the day I met my Messiah."

Emily (Lichtenstein) Seemar's Memories of Camp Tel Hai

There were various things that Ruth did at camp to make things fun. She would put Vaseline on doorknobs or come in the middle of the night and put the lights on saying, "I can't sleep, and nobody else will either." One year, Ruth acted as the camp nurse. I had some sort of asthma that year. Ruth was a wonderful nurse. No matter what ailed a person, Ruth prescribed "Absorbine Jr.," which is used for sore muscles. She would rub it on her "patient."

Beth Sar Shalom (House of the Prince of Peace) was the name that Chosen People Ministries gave to their summer camp. At the time that I was attending the camp, the ministry used the campgrounds of Camp Tel Hai in Honey Brook, Pennsylvania, fifty miles west of Philadelphia. We had the boys' cabins and the girls' cabins. Ruth was always there with the girls. We slept in rustic-looking cabins in bunk beds. We had hours and hours of great Bible study. Whatever Ruth told us to do, we did and loved every minute of it. We would have morning devotions before we had breakfast. Everybody would pick on Ruth at the breakfast table. We used to have this saying where all of the kids would loudly shout, in unison, "Miss Wardell, strong and able, get your elbows off the table!"

When we were lined up for any meal, Bill Ennis or Ruth would always sing these silly camp songs, which the kids loved and loudly joined in the chorus. Mealtime was always a joyous time of singing, having fun, and good fellowship.

Children came from Chosen People Ministries stations in Philadelphia, Pittsburgh, Coney Island, and Long Island (Levittown, Huntington Station, Brooklyn, and Queens). Between breakfast and lunch, there were Bible classes and team verse memorization. At the end of the two weeks at camp, there would be a contest to see which group had memorized the most Scripture verses. The winning team would get this huge container filled with ice cream nicknamed, "The Kitchen Sink." Afternoon was recreation time when we could pick any activity that we wanted to do. At night, we would study again. We would also sing a lot. We always sang a lot of traditional hymns. There weren't many Messianic Congregations back then, so there wasn't any Messianic music as we know it today. Near the end of camp, there was always a skit night. Ruth and the other counselors would dress up in funny costumes and do these skits. When we came home from camp, my father learned that we had all come to faith. He saw that it was a lost cause to keep us from attending the mission, so he let us go. This began my teen years.

Shirley (Silver) Kaufman

I first met Shirley when she came to camp as a counselor. I always said (and still say) that she was the best counselor that we ever had in camp. She had a love for the children, was kind to them, and treated them very well. I always admired the work that she did. The children really appreciated her, and now in their fifties, they still remember her love for them. We became very good friends and kept in contact all throughout these years. Shirley came to our camp for six summers. She was attending the Moody Bible Institute as a student at that time.

Shirley (Silver) Kaufman Remembers

Where do I begin to tell you about Ruth Wardell? I first met Ruth in New York in 1962, when I was a summer missionary with ABMJ. I spent four weeks that summer as a counselor at Camp Sar Shalom. I continued in that summer missions activity for six years! Ruth was my mentor then and is now my friend. She is an excellent Bible teacher. She often used camp themes when we were at Camp Sar Shalom in the early '60s. I remember them well. Her teaching is the type that sticks with you for a lifetime.

Shirley Silver, Sandy Schoenblum, Sonia

One year at camp, she taught the Fruit of the Spirit (Gal. 5:22–23). Each morning she gave a lesson on one of the fruit—love, joy, peace, etc. The campers, as well as the counselors, were supposed to try to live that characteristic for an entire day. The first day we were to show love to one another, the second day joy, and so forth. I was doing fine until "meekness" day. I'll never forget it. I struggled all day to be teachable and meek. It seemed like Satan was there at every turn to trip me up and show me how UN-meek I was. I've never forgotten that day—and the lesson Ruth taught on meekness.

Another year at camp, the theme was "Keep Yourself Pure." Throughout the teenage camp, Ruth challenged the kids about living a pure life for Jesus. Ruth lived what she taught and often had a cute phrase to challenge us. One of my favorites was "Jesus be with you," which she shouted out when you left her.

At camp, she woke the kids up every morning with a cheerful but loud song:

Yawning in the Morning!

Yawning in the morning

When the big bell sounds its toll,

We've only had ten hours of sleep

And we would like some more.

Ohhhhhhhh . . . I wish we'd gone to bed

When the sun was setting red.

Then we wouldn't be yawwwwwwwwwning—

In the morning.

It was her trademark at camp. The kids moaned and groaned (and so did the counselors) but her voice singing that song still resonates in my brain. Over the years, Ruth has kept us all connected, both campers and counselors! This has been a great blessing.

Besides being an excellent Bible teacher, Ruth gave practical advice and wisdom. It was never with a "holier than thou" attitude but rather gentle and godly guidance. One of her passions was to live a balanced life. Her motto was "Are you practicing your SPEMS?"

SPEMS = Spiritually, Physically, Emotionally, Mentally, and Socially

Throughout her life she encouraged us to practice SPEMS. Unless you're balancing your life in these five areas, you are lopsided and off-balance. Over the years, when we would talk on the phone, she would ask me if I was practicing SPEMS. I would usually say, "Only in 2 – 3 areas." Sometimes I actually got four—but I never got them ALL!

Ruth was a wonderful mentor to me. When I first met her in 1962, I was fairly shy and unsure of myself. She believed in me and had me speaking in front of groups of people in churches in no time at all. She had high expectations for us, and we all strove to meet them. Several years ago, she told me that I was one of the best counselors at Camp Sar Shalom. Those words meant more to me than all the accolades I have received over the years.

She is also very kind and forgiving. When she faced some of life's "knocks," she got right back up and persevered. She never criticized anyone but always tried to understand where a person was coming from. One of her expressions was "Life is cumulative, so you'd better start early to build good stepping stones!"

Dan and Arlene Rigney

Dan and Arlene Rigney

From 1968 until 1970, Dan and Arlene Rigney served as missionaries with ABMJ in New York City. From 1970 until 1975, they directed the Baltimore branch. During their Baltimore ministry, they also served as camp directors of ABMJ's Camp Sar Shalom. They worked as missionaries in the Baltimore, Maryland, area for Ariel Ministries which was founded and is now headed by Dr. Arnold Fruchtenbaum. Dan and Arlene Rigney were the greatest faithful couple for missionary work that one could ever meet. They were diligent workers for the Lord and very godly people. [*Editor's note:* Daniel Rigney graduated to heaven shortly after the 2010 session of Camp Shoshanah, where he had served with Ariel Ministries for many years.]

Dan and Arlene Rigney Remember

Arlene Remembers

Ruth's mother and father chose the right name for Ruth because Ruth is a faithful friend. She has always been obedient to the call of God and has always been faithful to the Jewish people that He has given to her. I guess that my favorite verse is also her favorite, "Your people shall be my people," (Ruth 1:15a).

Dan and I did not work directly with Ruth until 1967, when we were asked by ABMJ to come and work in the summer camp. One night, we got together and had a nice, long talk with Ruth because we were new to Jewish mission work. We weren't even finished with our studies at Moody Bible Institute yet. We had a little previous experience working in a camp (Good News Camp), but here we were, working with only Jewish children. Ruth sat us down and gave us helpful information. What I saw in Ruth that summer was her enthusiasm with the children and her ever-present smile. This rubbed off on the kids, who just loved her—and we did, too.

Dan Remembers

Ruth has been such an encouragement to us in that she has never sought her own glory in the forty-one years that we have known her. She told us the good, the bad, and the ugly about Jewish missions. This was great preparation for all of the obstacles and things that we would encounter in this mission field. She told us of the quirks that different people we might work with had and how to deal kindly with them. That was extremely helpful, particularly with the children. Ruth really showed us that Gentiles could witness to Jews.

Ruth has always been there for us. There were some times when things were rough, and we became discouraged and wanted to quit. Ruth encouraged us to hang in there and to remember that God is faithful. This is in stark contrast to some of our other Christian friends, who had told us not to go into Jewish missions because we would never see any fruit.

Her motto is something that is very catchy but is also very true. She refers to herself and is known to many as "Ruth with the Truth."

CHAPTER 10
The Youth

In my earlier years with ABMJ, in the 1950s – 1960s, there were not many youth groups at churches for young Jewish believers to attend. There were hardly any Messianic Congregations that had been established. There weren't nearly as many Jewish believers then.

So, working with the teens became a challenge. It took a lot of time to plan programs for them where they could be nourished by the Word of God and grow spiritually. One of my joys was to take a group of teens on retreats to places such as Schooley's Mountain in New Jersey. This retreat was set at the top of this mountain, and it had the feel of a spiritual place.

Of all of my responsibilities, the teen group was one of my favorites. The young people really enjoyed the retreats that we used to schedule. If adults would go on one of these retreats, they might say that it seemed boring. There did not appear to be much to do. Compared to the video-game age of today, it might well appear that way. However, those children did not feel that way. They were happy because they were together. In the evenings, they would sit on the living room floor and play Bible games that they often made up themselves. They always had a great time.

In the afternoons we would go into town, Hackettstown, New Jersey. The young people loved being out in the open air, handing out tracts to the people they met on the street. We had a tract entitled, *Four Things That God Wants You to Know*. The children would hand the tract to a person and then ask, "Do you know the four things that God wants you to know?" No one ever knew the answer, so the children would tell the people the four things which explained how to be saved. The four things God wants you to know: 1) You need to be saved; 2) You cannot save yourself; 3) God has provided for your salvation; 4) The Lord Jesus is able to save and keep.

The group would meet every Friday night at the Old Williamsburg Mission to the Jews. They came from all over. There would be eighteen to twenty young people. Most were Jewish, and they all looked forward to these gatherings. Many came straight from school, and they would make food and have dinner together. That was their place. They took the old chapel and put shields on the windows to protect them from the ball that was flying around as they played basketball and other games. These were times of great fun for the young people. The evening was also full of Bible teaching, music, and prayer time. These young people loved to pray together, and the answers they received to their prayers were always a source of great encouragement. The young people just loved to be together. They had a special call on their lives which made them unique.

Messianic Youth Fellowship (MYF)

As young people entered their teens, they joined the Faith for Teens group, and as they got older, they became part of the Messianic Youth Fellowship (MYF). MYF was a group of young Jewish believers that came into existence in the mid-1950s. It was the only group of believing Jewish young people that met on a weekly basis in the entire United States during the 1950s and 1960s, and it became well-known as a result. Today, there are many more groups, but back then there were not many places for these young people to come together to fellowship. Both groups produced monthly newsletters which included news of the day, testimonies, and information that kept the youth informed of the activities for the month.

I remember how I used to pile seven, eight, or nine teens into my station wagon. I would take them to a church that had invited us to speak. I would take Faith for Teens, the younger group, out one Sunday evening, and the next Sunday, I would take the older, college-aged group, MYF. I would take them everywhere and anywhere. We went to New Jersey, Pennsylvania, Boston, Long Island, and even Washington, D.C. We often did not get home until 11:30 p.m. to 1:00 a.m. on a Sunday night, and not once did parents say that I was bringing their child home too late. Some of the parents were believers, and some were not, but no one complained. These were happy, wonderful times for the children. The young people would learn to speak before groups of people in churches, and they were received very well.

Most of the time, the young people would share their testimonies and describe what it meant for a Jewish person to come to faith. Herb Manitsky usually was the group's Master of Ceremonies. He would introduce each member. There was a girl named Barbara Mickus who was a great opener for the group. She would really get the people interested in what was to be shared. After Barbara finished, the others would come and give their testimonies. Sandra Schoenblum had a great sense of humor and was naturally funny. She would have the audience rolling with laughter. And to wrap things up, Arnold Fruchtenbaum would close the session. This group would feel happy and important as the members of the church would gather around them asking questions about their testimonies. Since this was a time when there were not many Jewish believers, churches were very blessed by the testimonies that they heard.

Fredda (Breslaw) Payne

I first met Fredda in 1957 – 1958 when I began working for ABMJ on Long Island. Her family had moved there from the Bronx. Being Jewish believers, they were very happy that ABMJ was there on Long Island, and they became involved with the mission. Fredda's father led the mission meetings on Long Island, and her mother taught the children's classes. I have known Fredda since she was a young girl. She grew up in the classes and then grew into the teenage group. She was always a joy to be with. She needed Jewish fellowship because she had been brought up in a very Jewish-oriented extended family of believers. Her parents had a background in the mission. When the family suddenly moved away from the mission, Fredda did not have that fellowship. When we came and established missions on Long Island, Fredda and her family were thrilled.

Fredda has been a great believer, and she is very much involved in church ministry at this time. Her love for Jesus is very strong. She is just a pleasure to be with.

Fredda (Breslaw) Payne Remembers

My parents met at ABMJ in 1937. My father, Louis Breslaw, was brought to the mission in 1930 by his mother as a young boy. My great-grandmother also came to the mission. My father told me that they both made professions of faith. My father and his six brothers and sisters all came to faith. My mother, Harriet, began attending in 1937 when she was around sixteen years old. My father began years before that. It was here that they met.

Fredda

When I was very young, we lived in the Bronx, New York, from 1952 to 1956. My mother would take me to nighttime meetings in Brooklyn on Throop Avenue under the el train. [*Editor's note*: The el train is "the elevated train." This is a subway that ran some thirty feet above ground in the outer boroughs of New York City.] My father would meet us there after work. I also remember my mother's taking me during the day to weekly women's meetings at the 72nd Street Mission in Manhattan. When we would come into the building, my mother would take me immediately into the basement where she would leave me with my teacher, Miss Hilda Koser. I remember that this was more than just babysitting. As young as I was, I remember learning, "Jesus Loves Me," "Running Over," and other songs and lessons.

I went to the mission on Sundays with my parents and my sister. Then around 1955 or 1956, my family moved to Long Island. My parents wondered what they would do as far as coming to the mission. We lived too far out on Long Island to commute back and forth to Brooklyn every Sunday. The people at the mission told my parents to find a local Baptist church because they had similar beliefs. My parents couldn't see themselves going to a church. They had always attended the mission on Sundays. My parents looked around for a church, and after much searching, they finally found one. The church they found was Northport Baptist Church in Northport, Long Island. We attended this church for about seven or eight years. To a little kid like me, this seemed like an eternity.

Interestingly enough, I never equated the church with the mission. In my mind, these were two distinct bodies. There was church and then there was the mission. In church, one had Sunday School and then the big church service. We learned the same songs that we had already learned in the mission. Sunday School in the church was a bit different than the Bible School at the mission. At the mission, we learned more about the Old Testament books than we did at the church. I was aware that this was all about the same God. I did receive good teaching in both places. However, I would have preferred to go to the mission. Every once in a while, we would go into the city to attend a mission meeting.

When I was young the mission had classes in Levittown. There were Friday night meetings. We would all go as a family. This is where Miss Ruth Wardell comes in. She was the children's teacher in Levittown. I remember being taught Bible stories by Miss Wardell at Clara Rubin's house in Huntington Station, and I attended there on Monday afternoons. Soon thereafter, in 1957, we started having monthly meetings in Westbury, Long Island, for the whole family on Sunday afternoons. We would attend church on Sunday mornings, and once each month, we would go to the meeting held by Chosen People Ministries. This was called the "Friend's Meeting House." Those were great meetings. Those were fantastic times. We would share a meal. We would gather and sing, and then the children would go down to the basement where Miss Wardell was waiting for us. She would lead us in song, play games, and most importantly, she would teach us the Bible.

Miss Wardell would take us to churches where we would give our testimonies about how a Jewish child came to faith in Jesus. She would also take us on many retreats but there were preconditions. In order to go on a retreat, one had to memorize a certain number of Scripture verses. It seemed like I had to learn 1,000 verses. It actually was far fewer than that, but to me that's what it seemed to be. The mission covered most of the costs, but we also had to earn money to go on a retreat. She taught us responsibility and what it meant to work for something that we wanted.

Nothing is easy with Ruth Wardell. When I was eleven years old in November 1962, I told her that I wanted to get baptized. She agreed and gave me a package of papers that she made up with the requirements for being baptized. I had to research Bible verses, memorize verses, and I had to do a Bible study, among other activities on the list. Everyone who was baptized with me had to fulfill all of these requirements as well. I was baptized by Daniel Fuchs at the 72nd Street Mission in Manhattan. Ruth was there that day and has pictures of us in our little baptismal gowns.

Ruth and I are still friends today. To this day, I remind Ruth of her requirements for baptism. When I am planning to visit with her, I ask her if there is going to be a list of requirements that I will have to fulfill before spending time with her. She knows exactly what I am talking about, and we laugh about it. However, it was a great way to learn. Miss Wardell was exactly what a kid like me needed growing up in the 1960s. There was never a time that we would be with her that we did not have a Bible study. She taught us how to have godly fun as well. To be sure, the times we spent with Miss Wardell were anything but dull. This was very, very important to me as a teenager because I just never seemed to fit in with the youth group at my church. Being with other Jewish believers was a more comfortable situation for me when I was a teenager. I am so grateful for that because I needed that fellowship.

Ruth would also take us on "Mystery Outings." She would load us into a car and just drive. We always knew that she never knew where we would end up. This trip was a mystery to her as well. Whenever we would have a party, there would always be a theme. One time, we had an animal party where we all had to dress up as animals. We tore up newspapers to make a shredded paper floor as they do in pet stores for the pets. I can't believe that people allowed us to do things like this in their homes, but they did.

Life moved on. I went to college and got married. We lived on Long Island. Miss Wardell had moved on to California and then "retired" to Texas. Occasionally, we would get to see Miss Wardell when she would visit Long Island. The few times she was on Long Island allowed her to develop a strong relationship with my son Charles. They just seemed to hit it off. From the time that he was five or six years old, she would teach him things and play around with him. She always liked to tickle the children, and my son was no exception. Of course, Charles would want more. She used to do the same thing to us even into our teen years. You have not been tickled until Miss Wardell tickles you. After she returned home, I would speak with her by phone. While he was still young, my son would always ask to speak to Miss Wardell.

Then we moved to Florida. My dad had passed away when my son was twelve years old. Charles didn't want a Bar Mitzvah since his grandfather had died. There were only nine months left before he turned thirteen years old in October 1999. Suddenly, from out of nowhere, my son told me that he changed his mind and now wanted a Bar Mitzvah. There is a great amount of studying, practicing and preparation for a Bar Mitzvah. What could we do on such short notice? When I was speaking to Ruth one day, she told me that she was going to be in Gainesville, Florida for a meeting and then afterwards, she was going to come to my house to visit. I told her about my son's change of heart, and she told me that there was no problem and that I should not worry. She changed her flight and stayed with us, which was a real treat. She started teaching Charles the Hebrew language. Since she was only able to stay for a few days, we videotaped her saying the blessings in Hebrew so that Charles could watch the tape and learn these prayers by playing the tape over and over. For the next nine months, Charles and Miss Wardell would be on the phone constantly. She had given him a book to study Hebrew. For hours at a time, they would review the lessons that he had done. Finally, he learned sufficient Hebrew over the phone to be able to recite his Torah portion and the prayers for his Bar Mitzvah.

Charles Payne – Bar Mitzvah

The next hurdle to overcome was finding a location for Charles's Bar Mitzvah. Most Jewish congregations would not consider allowing the Bar Mitzvah of a Jewish believing family to occur in their synagogues. We asked our pastor if we could celebrate the Bar Mitzvah proceedings in our church. He said that he would love to have that take place in the church.

Miss Wardell arrived a few days early to help with the preparations and to review the prayers, etc., with Charles. Charles had a glorious Bar Mitzvah. Ninety-nine-point-nine percent of the people in attendance were Gentiles. There was one Messianic Jew invited, and he said that this was the best Bar Mitzvah he had ever attended. People were very moved by the speech Charles gave, and Ruth heard him preach his first sermon. The youth minister played the piano. He had grown up in New York, and even Gentiles in New York know the joyous Jewish dance, the *hora (hoe-rah')*. He knew how to play "Hava Nagila" ("Let Us Rejoice"), the traditional *hora* music. He was also familiar with many other traditional Jewish songs played at this celebration. The people joined in on many of the songs and had a great time. I'm just happy that we could bring some Jewishness to the people and let them experience a bit of the culture that God used to bring Messiah to mankind. That day I felt that a bit of the mission was there.

Miss Wardell manages to get to Florida every other November for Thanksgiving with our family. This is a very special time for us because we all love her very, very much. Just by being around her, one can't help but learn things. I find that I am still learning from Miss Wardell just as I did all those years ago as a child. We'll be sitting around after dinner and she'll say, "Come. Let's go look at stars." And we will go and look at stars and get a great lesson about the stars and the Bible. Sometimes, when we are around her, we forget that she is a Gentile because over the years she has picked up a lot of Jewish mannerisms, phrases, and thought patterns. She sort of grew up in the mission herself, having started as a missionary when she was only twenty-two years old.

Knowing Ruth Wardell for these many years has been a blessing for me and my family.

Naomi Seidman

Naomi Seidman's Jewish parents became believers through the work of Hilda Koser in Coney Island in the 1950s. When Naomi was in her late teens, Hilda put her in contact with a Jewish believing boy in California. She was in New York, so they wrote back and forth to each other. Eventually, things worked well and they got married. They have three lovely children and many grandchildren. They are very fantastic Jewish believers, and they have worked in churches to help Gentile believers warm up to Jewish people so that they may go out and share the Gospel with Jewish unbelievers.

Naomi Seidman Remembers

After living in the Bronx and Queens, my Jewish believing family moved to the Coney Island section of Brooklyn in the fall of 1953 when I was almost thirteen. It was there that we were introduced to ABMJ, also known as Beth Sar Shalom. In recent years, it has been renamed Chosen People Ministries.

Naomi Seidman

In the summer of 1954, I piled onto a bus with other kids to go to Camp Sar Shalom. Except for a hospitalization when I was about eight, this would not only be my very first camp experience, but also my first time away from home. The moment I sat down on the bus, I began getting a queasy feeling in my stomach. It wasn't the motion sickness to which I was prone, but rather homesickness. I hadn't even left Coney Island and had already decided that I would not be able to survive the two weeks away from my family. The camp was in Connecticut. I recall the bus taking us to a train station, where we boarded a train that took us out to the country.

At the station, we met with other teenagers from the Brooklyn Mission branch and proceeded to our destination. Despite the fact that I had a few friends from Coney Island when we started and met some new ones from Brooklyn by the time we arrived at camp, there was no place I would have rather been than at home!

Our luggage was dropped off in the dorms, and then we went to the mess hall for dinner. My stomach was in knots, and eating was the last thing I wanted to do. Then we arrived at our assigned tables—and there she was, Miss Wardell! We never referred to our counselors and teachers using their first names. I actually did not call her Ruth until many years later. With her keen insight, she may have noticed how upset I was because she wasted no time putting me at ease. When she found out that my name was Naomi, she shared that her first name was

Ruth and immediately began calling me her "mother-in-law." This is a practice that continues up to the present time. By calling me her "mother-in-law," she got me laughing, and laughter is good for the soul. I soon began to relax and was thrilled to know that this wonderful lady who showed me such love and understanding was going to be my camp counselor for the next two weeks.

I was so impressed with what Ruth could do. She led our song time by playing her accordion and singing out with gusto. I can still hear her voice whenever I sing certain gospel hymns. Then, she would scare us with ghost stories in the dark dorm rooms. We loved them. Yes, even I loved the scary stories. She would also lead our prayer times and give some of the lessons. That was the summer I gave my heart to the Lord Jesus. I was certain we had the best counselor in the entire camp.

As the years progressed, I married a Jewish believer and moved to California. After a couple of years, we moved back to New York and lived in Valley Stream, Long Island, followed by a couple of years living in Bethpage. Ruth and her dear, sweet mother lived close by in Levittown, and I often went to Bible studies at their home. After two of our children were born, Ruth would occasionally watch them upstairs in her bedroom so that I could enjoy the study being taught by Ruth's very good friend Eleanor Bullock. Ruth not only watched the children, but she used the opportunity to teach them about the Lord. By 1967, my husband and I decided to move back to Southern California. Not too many years later (1973), Ruth also moved there, and we got to see each other from time to time. It was always a blessing to have her come to our home or to go to hers.

If Ruth spent a weekend with us, she'd come to our church. Once, when we were turning around to shake hands and greet others in the pews, Ruth began telling the lady behind her that she was there with her "mother-in-law" and pointed to me. Since Ruth is seventeen years older than I, the woman kind of looked back and forth at us with an odd expression. A bit embarrassed, I attempted to explain that it had to do with our Biblical names, but it seemed too much for the lady to take in, so she probably went on thinking that Ruth had robbed the cradle. Occasionally, we would see Ruth at a Jewish meeting, and once again she took part in teaching our children, especially our oldest son.

There was a birthday party for Ruth when she turned eighty. We weren't able to be there, but the party planners asked for memories about Ruth, and I wrote a poem. (See poetry at the end of the book.)

Emily (Lichtenstein) Seemar

Emily came to our mission station when she was a young child of about four years old. Her father was against her attending the mission, but she did come to classes with her mother. At camp one summer, she accepted the Lord. When she left home to attend Bible college, things were such that she could not return to her home. She had nowhere to stay, so I told her that she could stay with me in Levittown, New York, for as long as she wanted. I fixed up a room for her to live in for as long as she needed. It became a place of refuge for her while she was in her college years. It was difficult for her to grow up with so much uncertainty in her life. Having her own room gave her some sense of stability. As a result of that time together, we grew very close and are still close to this day. We call each other a couple of times each week. In fact, Emily and her husband Bob are working as missionaries for Chosen People Ministries.

Emily

The first year at Bible college, she was always getting pink slips which were given when a student was not heeding the rules. I used to joke with her and suggest that we could paste them on the wall of her room as wall paper since she was getting so many of these disciplinary referrals. I guess she was trying to find herself at that time of her life.

When Emily started her second year of college, she had already met Bob, and I could see that she really liked him. I suggested that maybe she could give up the pink slips. I told her that she had had her fun. One year was enough. I also suggested that she probably owed the dean an apology for all of the hard times she had given her. She did settle down and did very well in her courses. She married Bob, and now they are both in mission work. Emily and her family often came to visit with me down through the years. These visits were very joyous and happy occasions.

Emily (Lichtenstein) Seemar—Memories

My mother was the first to meet Ruth Wardell. Mother came to faith when I was about four or five years old. My sister and I began to attend the Long Island Mission. A few years later, we met Ruth, who was working with the children. As a little girl, I remember this tall, tall woman with a booming voice. She was not frightening to us, but she was joyful, cheerful, and so much fun. All of the kids absolutely loved her.

My family had been going through difficult times, and there hadn't been a lot of joy in our home. Ruth's outgoing, joyful personality was in stark contrast to the mood at home. Both of my parents were Jewish, but my father was not a believer. He did not object to my mother's attending the women's classes because he felt that she needed that kind of activity. As my sister and I grew, we started hearing about Jesus, the Jewish Messiah. When that happened, my father forbade us from attending any more classes. He did not stop my mother from attending, but he did not want his two daughters and son exposed to any teaching about Jesus. Occasionally, we would attend a Bible class.

My father had been raised in a very religious home where education was encouraged. Unfortunately, the more education he received, the further he was from God. By the time my siblings and I arrived on the scene, my father was an agnostic (one who does not admit or deny the existence of God). He wanted the family to go to a little synagogue in Levittown, but they required giving to a building fund which he did not want to support, so we did not attend. Even though my father was not a practicing Jew and a self-described agnostic, he still felt very strongly about *not* wanting us to become traitors to the Jewish people by becoming believers in Jesus. He saw Jesus as the God of those people who had persecuted Jews throughout history.

Ruth Wardell came to our house for my birthday one year. I was thrilled. Ruth was like a movie star to us. Birthdays were never a big deal in my family. Ruth came and brought a present. To this day I remember opening that present and being excited and thrilled that she had come to celebrate my birthday. We were so hungry to find out about Jesus. Ruth was so wonderful in her Bible class. She made the Bible come alive for anyone who listened to her teach about the Gospel.

When I was nearly twelve, my father allowed us to go to Camp Sar Shalom, the summer camp run by Chosen People Ministries. He knew what the camp was about, but there was no fee for going, and he could not have sent us to another camp since he could not pay for it. It was at this camp that I came to faith. Of course, Ruth was there. Her love for children and the way she understood and worked with us was wonderful. You know, Ruth is really just a big kid at heart.

Emily on the Youth

Throughout my teen years, I was part of a group that Ruth discipled. As teens we did much together that really solidified us as a group. It meant so much to us to get together since it was rare to find many Jewish kids who believed in Jesus. When we were together, we were with like-minded friends. On Wednesday afternoons after school, we would have meetings at Ruth's house. On Friday nights, we could go with Ruth to the Friday night meetings in Queens where we could meet up with other Jewish believing youth. We were hungry for the things of God, and we could never get enough. We were like sponges, soaking up as much as we could about Jesus and enjoying times of fellowship.

One year, my high school in Levittown was hosting a concert with *Johnny Maestro and the Brooklyn Bridge*, a popular singing group. I didn't usually go to a lot of the school's activities, but this concert was of great interest to me. I struggled about going since the concert was scheduled for a Friday night, which was one of our meeting nights. Should I go to this concert or go with Ruth to our meeting? I so enjoyed these times with the group that I thought that maybe I shouldn't go to this dance/concert. I finally followed my heart and decided to go with Ruth to our meeting. This was not because I was so holy, but rather because these times meant so much to me and to the other Jewish youth that believed in Jesus.

When we were teens, Ruth would get invitations from churches for the group to come and speak to the congregants. We would share our testimonies. This was always well received by the churches. Keep in mind that, back in the 1960s, there were virtually no Jewish believing youth groups, and Jewish believers were few and far between. Ruth helped us to put together a program. We would begin by singing upbeat songs. There was a song, "The Light of the World is Jesus." We changed the lyrics slightly and renamed it, "The Light for the Jew is Jesus." Then we would share our testimonies. We sang and spoke at churches here and there in the New York area. One time, we were even invited to a church in Boston.

Our group was well organized. We would elect officers to run the group activities, and we had a newsletter/magazine, entitled Faith for Teens. We would write articles about different topics of faith as well as writing about our experiences. This provided a wholesome group where we could feel accepted. Teens need to belong to a strong foundational group.

One fantastic provision of the Lord was the knowledge that the mission was always there to go to. It not only was the instrument by which I found my Messiah, but it also provided a whole way of life for me, in which I could find guidelines for growing up. There is something about Hebrew Christian fellowship that draws you back like a magnet. I found an identity within this group that I could never have found elsewhere, especially in my teen years. It provided a social life for me in which all of the many outings and activities always had an emphasis on Christ and always bound us closer as a group.

Ruth was quite practical with the Scriptures and in the advice and counseling that she gave. The word that describes Ruth is *wise*. Ruth not only knows the Scriptures but she knows how and when to apply it. She sensed what the young people she worked with needed and then provided it. She always allowed the young people to be themselves.

Ruth had these easy-to-remember, profound lessons for us. She would have a sign with the letters **T-N-K.** This was a reminder for us not to say anything unless it was **T**rue, **N**ecessary and **K**ind. There were Scripture verses that supported this idea that we would memorize. Ruth made sure that these life lessons were brought down to a practical level. This was important so that we, as teens, could easily understand and remember these standards. We were maturing in the late 1960s, and these were socially and culturally turbulent years in the U. S. Rebellion was becoming well established with people my age, and if I didn't have the

Lord and Ruth, I'm sure that I and others would have been caught up in some of these behaviors.

She was a great encourager to many people. Ruth focused on my strengths and positive attributes and was always quick to tell me when I had done something well. This built up my confidence. If she felt that you had a talent for something (and Ruth believes that everyone has a talent for something), she would encourage you to continue using and developing that talent. My teen years were richer as a result of Ruth Wardell's being part of my life. The Jewish believing youth stuck together because we only had each other. It is significant to understand that we had each other because of her.

When we had a car full of kids, and we would be stopped at a railroad crossing for a few minutes to allow a train to pass, she would yell out, "Chinese Fire Drill." The next thing we knew she would turn around and begin to tickle everyone. Ruth has long arms, and no one escaped this tickling. It got to the point that any time we saw that we were going to be stopped at a crossing, we would all jump out of the station wagon so that she could not catch us.

When I graduated high school, I attended Northeastern Bible College in Essex Fells, New Jersey. I really wanted to learn the Bible, and I knew that if I didn't attend a full-time Bible college, I would never do it on my own. I also met Bob Seemar, my future husband, at this school.

Israel Trip, 1972

In 1972, while I was attending college, ten or twelve of us went to Israel with Ruth. We met up with Arnold Fruchtenbaum. This was one of the first tours that Arnold led in Israel. We were "tenting" everywhere we went. It was a great time.

I didn't come home from college very often in those days. By that time, I had come to call Ruth, "Mom." She was a great source of comfort and advice to me. There was an extra bedroom in her home, and she told me that that was my room whenever I wanted it. When I would go there, we would spend hours and hours just talking. She treated me like the adult that I had become. She showed me that working in ministry is not always easy and, in fact, many times it is a struggle. People are not perfect, and they can cause problems. I saw how Ruth dealt with those problems through these conversations. This prepared me for the disappointments and let-downs that a missionary often encounters.

In 2001, my husband Bob and I decided to go into full-time ministry with Chosen People Ministries. Bob owned a successful construction business. Working for the ministry requires that we speak in different places. I had spoken in front of groups ever since I was a teenager. Since public speaking was somewhat new to Bob, we would always speak together, which made Bob feel more comfortable. Oftentimes, when we were traveling to speak somewhere, Ruth would call us to encourage us and to build our confidence. We felt that we were never out there alone. Most importantly, Ruth would always pray for us and with us. Ruth is a real prayer warrior.

Emily and Bob

When Ruth says that she is going to pray for someone, she means it. Even when she says grace before a meal, one can hear the sincerity of her prayer. I'm still intimidated to say grace in front of her. For a lot of people, saying grace is thanking God for the meal and the food, and that's about it. When Ruth says grace, she thanks God for all that He is doing in her life and the lives of the people sharing the meal with her. Every prayer is detailed, personal, and unique.

Ruth has been and always will be an important part of my life.

Louis P. Viegas

This is the testimony of Louis P. Viegas from *Ha-Adouth* (The Witness), January-February of 1970:

> When I became interested in the work of the mission, I was a lost and discouraged soul. Unlike most of those in the Messianic Youth Fellowship (MYF) I am not of Jewish background, but came, instead, when I started to keep company with my wife, Sonia. I was born and baptized into the Catholic Church and even studied for a time to become a priest. However, I became more and more disillusioned the more I studied the Catholic religion and realized how much was "locked away" from the common Catholic person because the church did not think that the individual should interpret the Scriptures himself, but should be told what is right and what is wrong.
>
> After much soul-searching, I decided that I just couldn't believe in such a God and began a long search. After attending a few of the men's classes in Brooklyn, in the old Brooklyn building, I began to hope

anew, and in October of 1967, I discovered and professed belief in Jesus Christ as my personal Saviour.

Ruth's Comments

Louis married Sonia, who was also a member of MYF. Both of them were a great blessing to many in the mission. Sonia did a lot of teaching in the mission's children's classes. Both Sonia and Louis were very excellent counselors at our summer camps.

Cookie Schwaeber-Issan

Cookie

Cookie came to the mission when she was about thirteen years old. She was with me when I was in the Queens area of the mission. We used to have lots of Friday night meetings there for the teens. Her mother was a very wonderful believer in Jesus. She brought a lot of warmth to our mission station because she was outgoing in her faith. Her father used to act in some of the plays that we would present at the mission. We would laugh a lot and have a lot of fun while we were sharing the Word of God with people. Cookie wanted to go to live in Israel. This was a desire she had for all of her life. She studied Hebrew before she went to live there. Cookie got married and had a son. Sadly, just after they moved to Israel, Cookie's husband passed away. She persevered and now has remarried and is a grandmother. She has blessed many with her ministry in Israel.

Cookie Schwaeber-Issan Remembers

Ruth was our Faith for Teens leader, and it's fair to say that she was a singularly unique woman. There are so many humorous memories. I remember one of the many outings planned by her for us kids who were fifteen to seventeen years old. Bob Gross, one of the youth leaders, was much younger than Ruth. However, he had trouble keeping up with her energy and stamina. Once, we went on a trip to Storm King Mountain on the west bank of the Hudson River in New York State. We climbed straight up that mountain for hours, and I recall Bob saying, "Wardell has pulled some real stunts, but this one takes the cake." We just roared with laughter when he said that because we knew that he could not believe that she would make all of us climb up this mountain.

Ruth always seemed to have as much fun as we did. She never made us feel as if she were on another level. She was someone in whom we could always confide, someone we could always talk to, always receive guidance from, and with whom we could laugh. She was extraordinary in that way. She planned some of the most enjoyable outings for us and made sure that we always did interesting, active, healthy things. Ruth served us joyfully, lovingly, and with all her heart. There is no doubt in my mind that a great reward awaits her in heaven for her sacrificial life—a life that few in ministry today are really willing to devote. Ruth never aspired to wealth or fame. What she did, she did quietly and with no fanfare. In truth, she deserves all the accolades that can be given. She remains an inspiration to me as a real woman of God whose life meant something to so many of us.

Ruth's Memories of Herb Manitsky

Herb Manitsky's mother was a very strong Messianic Jewish believer. We called them Hebrew Christians back in the 1940s. Herb's mother attended the Old Brooklyn Mission, so Herb was in the mission before he was even born. Herb, along with his brother and sister, came to the mission regularly. It was a part of their lives. Herb was the youngest of the siblings, and he accepted the Lord at an early age. He was always involved with the mission and its activities.

Herb Manitsky

Herb graduated and became a soldier. He was sent to Vietnam, where he had a very hard time and came back very discouraged.

Of course, while he was there, he stayed in communication with the friends that he had made in the mission. He returned from the Army, married, and had two children. Today, he is working for a large Christian publishing company. He also served as a leader of the Messianic Youth Fellowship.

Herb Manitsky Remembers

Emily—"Peg Leg"

Ruth Wardell would always have some nickname for her "kids." Mine was "Herbite" because I was once bitten by a snake at ABMJ's summer camp in Honey Brook, Pennsylvania.

She named Emily (Lichtenstein) Seemar, "Auntie Em" (of *The Wizard of Oz* fame) but changed her nickname to "Peg-leg Charlie Brown" when she broke her ankle.

Ruth has always been upbeat and encouraging to us. She has a servant's heart and a passion for youth.

I fondly remember the trips. Once, she took us to Washington, D.C., to visit the Millers, Robert and Althea, who worked for the mission. We gave our testimonies in a church in Washington. There were also fun trips. Once, Ruth took the youth group to Jones Beach. I still have the sunspots on my neck and back from the horrible sunburn that I received that day. I will never forget the camping trip to Montauk Point, which is at the end of the south shore of Long Island. It rained so hard that I got soaked to the skin. We dried my pants on a grill and burned them. I wore burnt grilled pants all the rest of that weekend. We sure had fun!

I once told Ruth that whenever I hear the song "Thank You for Giving to the Lord" by Ray Boltz, I think of her. This is because of her great love for Jesus and her love for her "kids." I love you, Ruth.

Chaim Urbach

Chaim Urbach's family was originally from Europe. Around the time that the Nazis rose to power in Germany, Chaim's family moved to South America to escape the ever-increasing persecution. This was at a time when Jews could still leave Europe. They were some of the European Jews who foresaw hard times ahead, so they relocated. Chaim's parents became believers after they arrived in South America. Soon, they moved to Montreal. Chaim's father joined up with ABMJ, and the family then moved to New York to work with the mission there. Chaim's father worked for the mission for many, many years.

Chaim was also a very active member of the youth group that we had at the mission. Chaim, along with all of the others, really enjoyed the fellowship of the other Jewish believers. In the group, he had found some Jewish friends that he could relate to. When he first attended the youth activities, he needed fellowship, and this group welcomed anyone who wanted to join with them. It didn't matter who you were, where you were from, what you looked like, etc. They opened their arms and their hearts to all who sought to join them.

Chaim now leads a Messianic Congregation in Colorado.

Testimony of Chaim Urbach

From *Ha-Adouth* (The Witness), September-October of 1971:

> I was born into an average Israeli family. Both of my parents, while having a reverence for God, attended synagogue infrequently. Both were born in Poland and had many of their relatives killed in Hitler's holocaust.
>
> A few years after I was born, our family immigrated to Brazil due to economic reasons. There, my parents came across a group of very warm and loving people who claimed to follow Jesus Christ. Up to

that time, Jesus' name was anathema to both of my parents. From childhood, they associated with that name much of the suffering that our nation had to bear. That Person (Jesus) seemed to be completely foreign to them. However, the more they studied the Tenach (the Word of God, also known as the Hebrew Scriptures/Old Testament), the more they realized that Jesus could be no one else but Israel's promised Messiah.

Shortly afterward, we returned to Israel. There we joined a group of believers in the Messiah. There, as a child of twelve, I had an encounter with God. I placed my faith in Jesus as the atonement for my sins and thus entered into a new, personal relationship with God.

Chaim Urbach—More Memories

When I met Ruth Wardell, I was in somewhat of a culture shock. I had been born in Israel in 1950 into a family of Jewish believers. Our family moved to Toronto, where we lived for three years. We then uprooted and moved to New York City during the late 1960s. It was a very confusing time for me while I was in my latter teen years. The thing that impressed me about Ruth was that, in the 1960s, there didn't seem to be many people in the evangelical missions who really knew how to address issues with young people cleanly and with wisdom. I saw that Ruth was able

**Sarah, Chaim, and Eliezer Urbach
with Rachmiel Frydland**

to do that. She recognized that young people in their teens have hormones. Ruth didn't spiritualize that fact, nor did she condescend to the young people as others in mission work had done. She demanded a commitment to holiness and purity. It would be presented in a way that would catch the teens' attention. Things were kept simple with sayings and signs like, "Keep Yourself Pure" or KYP. Ruth understood that young people in their teens had all kinds of temptations *not* to follow KYP. The late 1960s and the early 1970s have been characterized as the beginning of the sexual revolution, so the temptations were becoming more socially acceptable. Ruth felt that she had to deal with the situation, no matter what the culture accepted as the norm. She kept it simple and direct—Keep Yourself Pure—until the appropriate time, which is marriage. This is the demand the Lord puts upon us, which is to walk in purity in the midst of all of that. Ruth made sure to talk to both the girls and the boys since they both needed to hear that demand.

I also was blessed by TNK, which stood for **True, Necessary,** and **Kind.** Ruth taught this to instruct people how to speak honorably about other people. By putting the ideas in easy-to-remember acronyms, the young people could understand the demands of the Scriptures in an easy, common-sense way. Before speaking, people should ask themselves if what they are about to say is **True, Necessary,** and most importantly, **Kind.** If one keeps to this guideline, one will not commit the sin of gossiping.

I also am impressed with Ruth's longevity in ministry. My father was a missionary for Chosen People Ministries, so I have seen mission work behind the scenes from the bottom up. This includes the good, the bad, and the ugly of Jewish ministry. In the Messianic Jewish movement, there are people who are involved in what can be characterized as a pioneering movement. As a result there are some who have a hard edge and are fighters who are willing to stand up to tremendous opposition. Not surprisingly, some of these people have been wounded and can seem harsh and uncaring, especially to a young teen. This is what I saw while growing up in the 1950s and 1960s. Ruth Wardell has been involved for sixty-three years and has not become jaded or cynical. She always had a sense of humor, and her love for the Lord and His Jewish people has not wavered.

Boston Trip

One of the trips that we took with the Messianic Youth Fellowship stands out in my memory. We went to a church in Boston. Our presentation consisted mainly of the young Jewish believers sharing their testimonies of how they came to faith. This time, the church congregation wanted to experience something authentically Jewish. The group decided to do a Yom Kippur (Day of Atonement) ritual that some Orthodox Jews practice called the Kaporot, which means "atonements." In this procedure, a live chicken (roosters for men and hens for the women) is taken and swung about one's head while a prayer is said, transferring the sins of the person onto the innocent chicken. The chicken is then slaughtered and given to a needy family for their pre-Yom Kippur meal. No food is to be eaten on Yom Kippur. We didn't know where to get a live chicken in Boston, so we did the next best thing. We went to a supermarket and bought a whole chicken. I took the chicken and swung it over my head and said the appropriate prayers. It was not exactly the traditional practice but it was as authentically Jewish as we could get.

Ralph Koffler—Memories of Ruth

Ruth Wardell played an instrumental part in my growing up. My mother, sister, and I lived in Levittown, Long Island, at a mission station for ABMJ. From childhood, adolescence, and then into youth, my sister Carolyn and I were involved in the different children's ministries under Miss Wardell's direction. There were weekly Bible studies, fun activities, interesting trips, and personal times with Ruth that gave us many special memories. Miss Wardell would pick us up on Friday after school and take us with her to the Brooklyn Mission in Williamsburg. There, we met other young people, became friends, and learned spiritual lessons through her love of teaching God's Word. The trip home from youth night was always filled with jokes, singing songs, and quick stops somewhere. We also knew that we would be found in Ruth's prayers. Our lives were changed by Bible classes, Christmas programs, and attending Camp Sar Shalom.

Reflections of Ruth will continually bring a theme of commitment to God and to others.

Joe Badalucca—Memories

Ruth was a large part of my life from fourteen to nineteen years of age. This was during the 1960s and 1970s. This period included the Vietnam War and the Hippie Generation. Ruth was a tall Canadian, Anglo-Saxon, bright-eyed, humorous single woman, serving her mission for Christ. Her flock was made up of children of all ages who were of Jewish descent.

Joe Badalucca

Ruth lived with her mother in the community of Levittown, Long Island, New York. Her home often served as the meeting place for the weekly meetings of the youth group. I will always remember how we laughed, prayed, studied the Bible, laughed, heard the Gospel message, laughed, praised the Lord, laughed, ate, laughed, played games, laughed, camped out in Ruth's backyard, and laughed. You get the idea—we loved these meetings. The young people enjoyed sharing these times with caring adults who treated us with dignity and gave us the attention that young people seek from adults. These Bible-believing adults also modeled appropriate behavior for us. Everyone was treated fairly and with respect. If a young person acted in an unacceptable manner, firm, even-handed adult authority was invoked. This was something that was usually lacking in our home life.

Ruth always drove a full-sized station wagon that seated nine to eleven young people. Ruth drove, and a horde of kids sat in the back, usually in the order that we were picked up and then dropped off. Friday night was when we had the Brooklyn Youth Meeting. The neighborhood of the Brooklyn Mission had become a rough neighborhood with much gang activity. This was the late 1960s and early 1970s, when New York City was experiencing racial tensions. One had to be careful about where one went in these neighborhoods. Ruth, however, had the Lord on her side, and I never once saw her flinch or fear the rough neighborhoods that we passed through to get to the Brooklyn Mission.

When we would arrive at the mission, Ruth would double park and unload the kids, food, and meeting supplies. All of this took place under the watchful eyes of the gangs hanging out across the street and on the corners. Once we unloaded the car and the kids were safely inside, Ruth and I would circle the block looking for a parking space. Once we parked, we would then walk back to the building. I was nervous walking these streets, but Ruth would talk to me and laugh and never once looked concerned. The Lord always covered her.

I believe that Ruth must have driven the most miles any missionary stationed in a foreign country had ever driven. She drove through blizzards, hurricanes, and heat waves. We always felt safe and happy. I spent hundreds of hours in station wagons with Ruth, and these were some of the liveliest, happiest times of my life.

Lyn (Rosen) Bond

Lyn (Rosen) Bond

Lyn (Rosen) Bond is a vivacious missionary with Jews for Jesus. She is the daughter of Ceil and Moishe Rosen, the founder of Jews for Jesus. She loves the Lord, and she's a very good witness of the Gospel. I first met Lyn at this camp in Cedar Lake, Indiana, when her father was teaching there at a prophecy conference held by Chosen People Ministries. She was one of the students in my class. She was about eleven years old then. I met her again when she was a teenager, and one time she assisted in summer camp. She moved out to California, and when I moved there in 1973, we met up once again. We used to go walking together. When I came to the Dallas area, we met up yet again as Lyn was living here doing work for Jews for Jesus. We have had a long-lasting relationship. I knew her father, Martin, before she was born. He had worked for Chosen People Ministries for many years before founding Jews for Jesus.

Lyn (Rosen) Bond—Memories

I first met Ruth in the 1960s. It was at a prophecy conference that my parents were attending in Indiana at Cedar Lake. Eleanor Bullock and Ruth Wardell were the teachers for the young people. I was maybe ten years old, and she was so welcoming of me. There was none of the attitude that her meal-time was her time off, so "Don't bother me kid." She would let me come and sit with her at meals, and she was genuinely happy to have me around. She has always been a Barnabas to me in that she has always encouraged me to be the person that God made me to be. She encouraged me to memorize Scriptures, which is one of her big things. I noticed that Ruth's method of disciplining children is unique. All of the years that I have known her, she has always had the same philosophy. She believes in disciplining children with love. When a little boy was getting out of hand, she would threaten him by saying, "Okay, now I'm going to kiss you." When a little girl was getting out of hand, she said, "Okay, I might have to tickle you." I have never heard Ruth raise her voice in anger. I have heard her get a little edge in her voice when enough was enough.

One time I was hit by a car and nearly lost my life. I was having some very down times. Ruth would call me on the phone to encourage me. I knew that the advice that she was giving to me was true because I had seen Ruth live through some very trying times in her life. I saw Ruth when her mother was dying. I saw her deal with serious medical conditions. I saw her deal with a broken foot. She dealt with all of these situations with joy. Of all of the emotions that one can choose during these times, Ruth always made joy her choice despite pain or restrictions on her mobility. She loves others because the Lord loves her, and she gives that love to others.

I'm in my fifties now, but when I was in my thirties and forties, I used to sincerely tell Ruth that I wanted to be like her when I got older. I wanted and still want to be encouraging like Ruth and have good things to say about other people. I want to be in the Word of God just like Ruth. I hope that I can have an open heart and an open hand to others like her.

It would be erroneous to say that Ruth is a woman who is without children. Ruth has more children, grandchildren, and great-grandchildren than you could mention.

Campus Crusade for Christ

In 1972, I decided to take nine of the youth to Dallas, Texas, to attend Campus Crusade for Christ. We drove from New York to Dallas in a van that we loaded with tents because we didn't have any money to sleep in motel rooms. We left New York and stopped in Philadelphia to pick up Larry Feldman. This young man had not been saved that long, yet he carried a Bible everywhere he went. He was excited about his faith, and it was exciting to have him along on this long drive to Texas.

We arrived in Dallas after a long, fun drive. Along the way, we were assaulted by cicadas that swarm just once every seventeen years. These bugs were everywhere. They completely covered the sky and us. Larry hated these bugs. They got into our tents, and we had to get rid of swarms of cicadas from our sleeping area.

Chosen People Ministries had a booth at this Crusade, which was being held in the Cotton Bowl Stadium in the Fair Park section of Dallas. Shortly after arriving in Dallas, we met up with Tom McCall, the head of the Dallas Center of CPM. We slept on the floor of the mission house. The next morning, the group went to the Campus Crusade for Christ and helped with the booth. We would answer the many questions that people had about Jews who believed in Jesus among other questions about the Lord. There were 45,000 to 50,000 people there. We made buttons to hand out to the people that said, "I'm a Jew for Jesus." These buttons just disappeared. They were taken by multitudes of young Jews who came to faith across the country in the revivals of the late 1960s and early 1970s. It was reported that some 6,000 to 7,000 Jewish young people had come to believe in their Messiah. Many of these were in attendance at this crusade. For me, it was a very inspiring time to meet so many new young Jewish believers.

This time heralded the rebirth of the Messianic Jewish movement in America. The final night that we were there, all of the groups gathered together. Each person would light a candle and then pass that candle until the entire place was lit up by candles. It was impressive.

We started home knowing that we were being pursued by a developing hurricane that was moving up the eastern seaboard. Unfortunately, we could not out-race the storm all of the way home. We had to stay in a hotel one night because the wind and the rain were too powerful for us to set up tents. We arrived home safely with the memories of a powerful crusade fresh in our minds and with a new fervor to serve the Messiah.

Passover Celebrations

During the 1960s and into the 1970s, mission work changed a great deal. As we read in the above article, there were many Jewish people who came to faith in their Messiah. These people were very interested in Jewish life and customs, so Jewish Missions started celebrating the Jewish Holy days. In the previous era, missions mainly used Messianic prophecies as a way to evangelize the Jewish people.

There were five missionaries working in the branches on Long Island and Queens. We worked together to prepare celebrations such as Passover, Chanukkah, Purim, etc. We would also invite Jewish people and their friends to attend. We held these celebrations in a restaurant and on one occasion in 1967 we had 402 people in attendance and 352 of them were Jewish of which fifty were not believers in Yeshua.

Many heard for the first time the true Biblical significance of the Passover.

These occasions were very festive. The restaurant supplied the different items that are used at Passover like Matzoh (unleavened bread), grape juice, salt water, hard-boiled eggs, parsley etc. We would do the regular Passover service, and then end up with one of the missionaries giving a message. One year the message was called "Behold the Lamb  of God." This message explained that Jesus the Messiah was the fulfillment of the Passover celebration in light of Jesus being the Passover lamb. Our teachings always plainly taught how to accept Jesus as their Savior.

After the Passover celebration and teaching two Jewish people came to faith in Jesus. On the trip home one of the mission workers led two other Jewish women to accept Jesus as their Messiah. There were many opportunities to share the Good News of Messiah when we followed up by contacting those who had attended this event. These folks coming to the Lord always made the banquet something that was very worthwhile in our service for the Lord. It was very exciting to say the least. P T L

CHAPTER 11
Balancing My Life

Mother Comes to Live with Me

My father was a tireless worker who was always planting churches and study groups. As a result, he did not have very much time for himself. One morning in 1958, my father became ill. He was diagnosed with a bleeding duodenal ulcer. He was taken to the hospital and had an operation. The doctor said that the operation was a success, but because his body was like that of an eighty-five-year-old man, he was not healing as well as they would like. Father was only sixty-eight, but all his life he had overworked, and as a result his body looked and responded like the body of a much older person.

Ruth and her Mother

My father died about two weeks later. He had lived his life for the Lord, and God had taken him home. He was much loved by all the pastors who knew him. My father was a man who started churches. He had just finished building one in the town of Brampton where we lived at the time. It was a small church, but at the funeral service, one half of the church was filled with pastors from all over Ontario who had come to love and revere him for all the wisdom he had demonstrated. I remember thinking at the time that it was rather sad that he died so young since he had so much wisdom to pass on to the younger pastors. Indeed, I find that this is so true, and I am thankful that I have lived to be eighty-five and that I am able to pass on some of the wisdom that the Lord has given to me over the years.

My mother was now left alone in her home. Since she did not drive, it became difficult for her. Thus, it was decided that she would come and live with me in New York. It was a big change for her. It became my joy to get to know her over the next twelve years. My mother came to live with me in Levittown when she was sixty-eight years old. For the first three months, I sensed that my mother was thinking that a missionary should be a little more sophisticated than I was. I was not the stereotypical missionary person at all. For those months, I thought that I should tone it down for my mother. That was not going to be possible because that just wasn't me. One morning, I came down the stairs shouting, "Is anybody up in this house?!?!" My mother didn't know what was going on. After a while, she got used to who I was and how I worked. She enjoyed every minute of the happy times that we had together. One time, when I was upstairs, she was talking to someone downstairs. I was able to hear her say, "My daughter doesn't act much like a missionary, but I like the way that she is." She just accepted me as I was.

My aunt, my father's sister, came to Levittown with my mother to live with us. The three of us were together in that house. After about a year or two, I became very depressed. Work at the mission was difficult, and many of the workers were frustrated and dejected by many disappointments. I had to do my work for the mission and then, when I arrived home, I had to care for my mother and my aunt. This didn't leave much time for me to just relax and unwind. Slowly, I found myself becoming depressed. This was not a clinical depression when a person withdraws from their everyday life. I was just becoming overworked and overwhelmed. I said to my good friend, Eleanor Bullock, "You're a little depressed, and I'm a great deal depressed, so we are going to have to see how the Lord is going to lift us out of this. When I find out how to do this, I'll let you know." We laughed about that, but the depression did not lift. When you feel this way you cannot function properly. I couldn't study or do my work. I was resourceful enough to be able to get people to assist me in completing my responsibilities. The depression was persistent. I thought that there had to be some answer for it. I would sleep for nine hours at night, but I was still very tired during the day. I went to sleep tired and woke up tired. I was tired all the time. I prayed and said, "Lord, I need help with this. I have no reason to feel like this. I am following You and doing Your will for my life. I'm happy about that, but there is something that I'm doing that must not be quite right."

I went to a store and found a book entitled *How Never to Be Tired* and thought that this might be good. I brought it home and read it cover to cover. The book said that I was probably tired and depressed because I was bored. I thought that this concept was interesting. I concluded that I must be bored. The book suggested that I should think of five things that I wanted to do, and then I should go and do them. The book stated that if I did that, my tiredness and depression would lift. Thinking Scripturally, I thought that Jesus had done some of those things. He didn't just do work, work, work. My life consisted only of working and taking care of my mother and my aunt. I made that list and did those things that I wanted to do and within one week I was 100 percent better. One of the things on that list was to learn how to play the piano better. I needed a teacher, but I had no money, so I began babysitting on the weekends. I made the necessary money, took my piano lessons and even bought a piano. I learned how to play the piano better since I had to play a lot in the mission. I went back to college for one course. Since much of my work was helping people, I thought it would be good to take a course in psychology. I also needed to exercise, so I made sure to get up early in the morning to walk before I went to work. Within one week, I was sleeping for seven hours without waking up in the middle of the night. When I woke up, I was not tired but rather I was full of energy. I had learned "R&R." I learned how to include rest and relaxation in my busy schedule. As a result, the joy came back into my life. I have been able to help many others who have suffered from this situation in their lives. When I would see someone becoming discouraged, I would ask them what they liked to do and then I would do that activity with them.

Sometimes, as a Christian, if you express that you are feeling a little depressed, others will look at you as if you have done something wrong. Basically, I had not done anything wrong, but rather I had not done some things that would make me feel better and give me a little variety in my life. That was a great lesson. From time to time, people will come up to me and say that I am so upbeat. Then they ask me how I can be so upbeat all the time. The answer is that I learned from these experiences.

I share this because in my years of mission work I have encountered many missionaries who think that they shouldn't be bored because they are doing the will of God. Even when doing the work of God, one must allow time for themselves. In the days of Joseph Hoffman Cohn, early in my career, I had come out of a staff meeting and was feeling down. Remember that I was brought up in a very legalistic home. Here I was, twenty-six or twenty-seven years old (1949/1950) and had never seen a movie. This day, as I left the 72nd Street Mission, I was down. I was walking along, and I passed a movie house. I don't remember the title of the movie, but it was about a little English boy and Queen Victoria. I walked around the block to consider my next move. I thought, "There would be nothing wrong with seeing a movie about Queen Victoria and this boy." I had to be sure that I wouldn't be doing something out of the will of God. I went into the theater and saw this most charming movie about this little boy who came into Buckingham Palace through the coal chute. He came up under the table where the Queen was and he told the Queen that since she would not come to visit him, he would come to visit her. That woke her up. The Queen's husband had died and she was isolating herself from most people. The whole story was adorable and touched my heart. When I exited the theater, I realized that all of those heavy feelings that I had when I walked into the theater were now gone. That's how God showed me that one must balance every hard experience you have with something pleasing to you.

Dr. Joseph Hoffman Cohn would tell us at some meetings that whatever we experienced in mission work or in life, we should always be sure not to become cynical. He had been that way at times in his life, and he told us that cynicism accomplished nothing but was in fact a negative influence on one's life. I remembered that lesson and when I woke up I would pray, "Lord, do not let me become cynical today." There are so many things in missionary work that can make you cynical. Once you become cynical, it is difficult to break out of it.

Cynicism takes away one's joy because the cynical person doesn't trust anybody, and one does not want to do anything because he or she feels it's all for naught.

The Lord uses small things to teach us lessons. I remember one time just after I started working in Brooklyn when I got on the bus to go home after work and realized that I was on the wrong bus. Work was hard, and I was young, and I didn't notice that the bus that stopped at my bus stop was not the bus that went to my apartment house. I thought that this was okay. All I would have to do is ride this bus to the last stop and when it turned around to come back I would stay on until I could get to a stop where I could get the right bus. On the trip to the end of the line I got interested in all of the neighborhoods that I had not yet visited. When I got off of the bus I felt better than I had when the trip first started. I learned that if you're feeling down, do something new and different from your usual experience. Just a little bus trip made all the difference in my attitude.

The Lord was always trying to teach lessons to me. I guess that I needed a lot of those lessons. I was a rambunctious child, and I needed to learn a lot of things. The Lord in His mercy would teach me things to help me to be a better person for Him.

Mother and I traveled a lot. We traveled cross-country one time. Someone in the ministry wanted to get an old car from New York to California. This was in the middle of the winter. They asked me if I would be willing to drive it there. I agreed and planned a trip around this. I asked my mother if she wanted to accompany me on this drive to California. She responded with a very enthusiastic, "Yes!" She was seventy-five years old at that time. We started out from New York, in a car that did not have windshield wipers that worked. When it started to snow, I found myself getting out of the car many times to clear the windshield. I decided that a route change was necessary, so I informed my mother that we would now take the southern route to California. This new route took us through North Carolina and we had the opportunity to stop at a place there where my mother had lived and served as a nurse for a year before she met and married my father. In those days, tuberculosis (TB) was a common illness. She had gone to a little town in North Carolina to care for those suffering from TB. We then continued south and went across the southern route to California. My mother had the greatest time doing this. She loved to travel. We went to Vancouver twice, to Ontario several times, to California and Indiana to visit my brother.

My mother was always an active woman, and she soon began teaching a women's class at the church we attended. Healthwise, my mother did well for a while, but eventually she got older, and her health deteriorated. I had my bedroom on the second floor of the house, and my mother was in a room on the first floor because she could no longer climb stairs. My brother had set up a buzzer system in the house. If my mother needed something, all she had to do was press the buzzer and I would respond. Every night, my mother would buzz me to come down to get something for her or to help her do something. We had gotten a hospital bed with the rails on the side to keep her from falling out of bed in the middle of the night.

She could not get out of this bed without assistance so she would buzz me and I would come down and lower the rails and help my mother.

This procedure began to wear on me after many weeks of running down to my mother three or four times or more each evening and in the middle of the night. I remember coming down the stairs saying out loud, "Now Lord, I have nothing left to give to my mother. I have absolutely nothing. I don't feel anything for anybody. I don't feel anything at all. I'm very tired and weary, but You have promised that when we are weak, You are going to be strong. Therefore, I am going to trust you for my strength." Every time, I was able to go into my mother's room and share love, kindness, and joy with her. It wasn't mine. It was the love, kindness, and joy of the Lord. God loves weakness because then He can be strong. It was such a lesson for me to learn. My mother could also feel the presence of the Lord, and she responded which made for happy times for both of us. When I would leave the room, I would say, "Thank You, Lord. You really came through. I feel so satisfied with what I was able to do while I was in the room with her, and I'm sure that You are satisfied as well. Thank You for that lesson that You taught me today." So I learned and often say, "God delights in weaknesses." Since that time, I've always realized that through all of this experience with my mother, God had something for me to learn.

One time, a woman came from Canada to assist me with caring for my mother. She was sort of a fuddy-duddy kind of person. She wanted to help my mother because my mother had helped her when her mother was dying. This woman had problems with her children. They were not giving her very much honor, and she didn't know how to handle things with them. As a result, her self-esteem was quite low. I would stay at home with my mother and send this woman to church. Over time, people referred to her as "Mrs. Wardell's nurse." Soon I noticed that her personality began to change. She spoke, stood and walked more confidently. I bought her a new wardrobe, and we were able to send her home looking like a real lady. When she came off the plane back in Canada, her family hardly recognized her.

Another time, a nurse that we knew from Canada came to help me with my mother. She was highly recommended, but she was from the "old school" that scolded older patients if they did not do something the way it should be done. I told her that we don't do things that way. If the patient does not do something right, then think of something that she does do correctly and tell her that was a good thing she did. It is not good to scold someone lying in bed. This nurse came with the old attitudes. By the time she left our home, she was a whole new woman. She was so excited about what she had learned in the Lord. Through all of these experiences, these people grew in the Lord. They ministered to my mother's needs, and they were ministered to as well.

In the twelve years that my mother lived with me, I never felt that I was outside the will of God. I felt very strongly that taking care of my mother was what God wanted me to do. I find it interesting that I never felt that strongly about many other things in my life. Even in the final years of my mother's life, when she was very ill and I was up most of the nights with her, I never once doubted. It never crossed my mind that I should be doing anything else. In fact, it was during this time that I really got to know my mother, and this period of time was the closest that I had ever been to her. When I was young, living at home, I was usually off doing my own thing. However, God gave me a great privilege during those twelve years of really getting to know my mother. She and I had twelve marvelous years together. She was like a Queen Victoria. She could set a table with crackers and milk, and you felt like you were in an elite house. Everybody loved her. She was not only my mother but a very wonderful, fantastic person. She was a great teacher, and she lived what she taught.

I never heard her say one unkind word about anyone. This was a good example for me. In the twelve years that she lived with me, we never had one unkind word with each other. What a blessing to experience about living God's way.

My mother spent her entire life growing in the Lord. Everyone who met her loved her. When she was eighty years old, my mother went home to be with the Lord.

Margaret Wardell (Ruth's Niece) - In Her Own Words

Margaret Wardell and Ruth 2006

My father is Harold Wardell, Ruth's older brother. Aunt Ruth has always been very special to me. I have many happy childhood memories of visiting Aunt Ruth in Levittown, New York, from my parents' home in Montreal. My first solo bus trip to New York was in 1962 when I was just eight years old. My little suitcase was stolen, but Aunt Ruth turned a negative thing around, and we had fun together shopping for new clothes!

My paternal grandmother was living with Aunt Ruth in Levittown. I can remember climbing up into the attic and playing in Aunt Ruth's home. I can remember bike riding, going swimming in the local pool, and visiting the Empire State Building. I remember playing my violin with Aunt Ruth's friend, Vivian, who played cello in a local high school orchestra.

In the early 1960s, I went with Aunt Ruth and some of her young mission friends on a fantastic camping trip to Washington, D.C., where we saw the Lincoln Memorial, the White House, and Arlington Cemetery. I even put my finger in the crack of the Liberty Bell! I always had a fun time whenever I visited Aunt Ruth.

In 1993, Aunt Ruth moved to Texas where she is enjoying a very active retirement. My husband and I wish our dear Aunt Ruth a very fulfilling, continued retirement, although Aunt Ruth has never retired—she has just changed her focus!

CHAPTER 12
The California Years
(1973 – 1993)

Work in California

[*Editor's note*: Ruth states that the name "Ruth with the Truth" came about when she was in California. In New York, Ruth was known as "Miss Wardell." It had to be "Miss Wardell" because, in New York, things had to be more structured and formal. However, in California, things were a little more loose and informal, so when the title "Ruth with the Truth" came about, it stuck.]

North Hollywood, California

From 1946 to 1973, I worked in Brooklyn, Queens, Long Island, and Manhattan. This was a period of twenty-seven years. While most people would call this a full career, I was just getting started. The next place I headed to was California. There, I worked in North Hollywood. The name of the mission in North Hollywood was Beth Sar Shalom. This translates as "The House of the Prince of Peace."

My friend Marge Masoomian relates how her son helped me move from New York to California.

Marge Writes

In 1973, Ruth was planning to move to California. My son, Charles, was going to drive a truck with all of her furniture in it to her new home. Ruth would follow him driving in her car. Everyone pitched in to load her furniture on that truck. A man named Fred Taylor, who was an expert at loading trucks, appeared almost miraculously. Ruth didn't know that he was coming to help, and she didn't even know who invited him. He packed and balanced the load perfectly. It was indeed a miracle from the Lord because no one had much experience in packing a truck.

I arrived at the North Hollywood Station in October 1973. The Center was in a good location to witness to Jewish people because of the Jewish bookstore that was on the same block. There were many Jewish people in the neighborhood. The storefront that the mission was housed in had a big side wall outside where we could advertise our meetings. The place was very visible, as it was on a very busy street where multitudes of cars came by each day, and many people came to shop, not only at the bookstore but also at the wonderful Jewish bakery across the street.

Richard Cohen

A man by the name of Richard Cohen was in charge of the Los Angeles division of the mission. This year, 1973, was the era of coffee shops. Richard Cohen had set up a coffee shop at the North Hollywood Center. Unfortunately, this came toward the end of the popularity of coffee shops, and not many people attended. Richard was moving to offices in another building, and he appointed me to be in charge of the two storefronts.

Richard had given me a place to work, and he told me to do whatever I felt was necessary to accomplish the work. As long as there were no major problems, he basically left me alone. I saw this as a creative challenge, and I was very happy. He never bothered me as to what I did. He never came and said that I was doing something wrong and had to change how I was doing things. I really appreciated this.

Richard had many great ideas. He had held some meetings in Van Nuys Baptist Church, and we had a Sunday School where all the Jews could come to their very own class. I believe that it is a great idea for Jewish people to come to church and go to a Sunday School class to study about their own Jewishness. This helps them maintain their Jewishness and not lose it in a Gentile church. Richard Cohen would hold big meetings in this Van Nuys church, celebrating the Jewish holidays of Hanukkah and Purim. Hanukkah is also known as the Festival of Lights that commemorates the rededication of the Temple and the oil that burned for eight days when there was only enough oil for one day. Purim is the story of the Book of Esther.

My Beginnings at the North Hollywood Mission

When I first arrived at the North Hollywood Mission (also called the Center) on October 1, 1973, it was around the time of the Jewish holiday of Sukkot. I thought that I had to do something with the window display. It looked quite empty. There was only one book there. I quickly constructed a miniature *succah*, which is the booth that the Jewish people stay in for this holiday, commemorating the travels of the Jewish people through the desert for forty years. During this period, they lived in temporary tents or booths. The word *succah* means "booth." I put some items around the *succah* and put up a sign. In looking at this new display, it occurred to me that there still was not much there, so I covered the entire window with plain paper except for a hole that I placed at eye level. This provoked many people to look into the window to see what was behind the paper. It was a great success.

Jewish Evangelism Seminar

Soon after I started working at the North Hollywood Center, we hosted a Jewish Evangelism Seminar and invited all of the nearby churches to attend, so that they could know how to witness to their Jewish friends. We asked them to pray for us. We wanted to develop a relationship with them so that we could work together to evangelize the Jewish people. I was aware that one could not just come into a neighborhood and start a mission without making connections with churches in the area.

Building a Mission

One has to build up a mission. It just doesn't happen by itself. We wanted to try to find some volunteers to work at the counters in our reception area. From this Jewish Evangelism Seminar the Lord provided many volunteers. Some eighty-five people attended and learned many things about Jewish people and how to share faith with them. Some came to help with the children, others to man the front desk and chat with the people who came in off the street.

When I first came to the Center, there were just bare walls with big old wooden chairs, which looked just awful. However, the Lord had something wonderful in mind when He, in His mercy, brought a lovely couple with a multitude of talents to share in the work. Their names were Mary and Ray Brummell. Both became involved and helped in many, many ways.

Mary Brummell

Mary was a fantastic volunteer. I always understood that when somebody had a talent, you let them use that talent. Mary was one of those people. I would tell her to do whatever she wanted to do. Then, I would offer to help her. I believe that this really gets a person's creativity flying. Mary organized and fixed up the four rooms that comprised the entire Center in North Hollywood. She brought in a whole lot of books. She organized and

Mary Brummel

categorized all of the tracts in a display that was easily perused. When someone visited the Center, information could be easily obtained. Mary even organized a lending library.

The Center consisted of two storefronts that were right next door to each other. To go from one storefront into the other, you had to go out one door, onto the street, and into the door of the next storefront. The two storefronts weren't connected. With the help of Mary Brummell, her husband and others, a door was installed in the front and another door in the back of the mission on the common wall so that we could pass from one storefront to the other without having to go out into the street. This arrangement would allow me to have a lot of fun with the children. I would chase some of the boys and if I caught one, he would get a kiss from me. The boys would run away through these doors back and forth from one store to the other, trying to avoid a kiss. There was one little chubby boy, who would all of a sudden stop when nobody was there, and I would catch him and kiss his little *punum*, which is Yiddish for *face*. Then he would run away, but he really wanted that kiss.

Mary and her husband did a lot of renovation in this Center. They built a small reception office in the very front of the Center to receive people so that they would not disturb any of the activities that were going on in the rest of the building. Mary's husband had to sell a prized rifle to get the money for the materials to build this little office space. People like this are people that God brings along. They were great believers and loved the Lord.

When they were finished wallpapering, painting, etc., the place looked just lovely. The Center was transformed from awful to magnificent. Ray did a lot of the work, and all one can say is that the Lord sent the right person for the kind of work that needed to be done to fix up the buildings. Mary organized the office, set up tract racks, and helped to line up the volunteer program. She also created window displays and changed them every three weeks. Mary did this for nine years. Wow!

These window displays were very attractive and also very significant in respect to the Jewish holidays and the nation of Israel. They were used of the Lord to bring in many Jewish people to chat about the Messiah, as well as a lot of Christian people who wanted to know something about witnessing to their Jewish friends. Hardly a day went by that there were not several people who came in and asked questions. It was always exciting to me to hear the volunteers tell of their daily experiences as they shared their faith with so many people. Amen! Praise the Lord!

Mary Brummell Writes

I'm very ill and unable to write you a long letter about Ruth. What I can say is that Ruth is a friend that comes along once in nine lives. She is always faithful, always caring, and always loving over many, many years.

[*Editor's note*: Mary passed away in June of 2008.]

CHAPTER 13
Ministry for
Senior Men and Women

One of the many focuses of the Center was work among seniors. We met on Tuesday evenings. Jean Ambro, Rose Mitchnick, Madeline Goldberg, and I all worked together in a wonderful fashion to make the meetings possible. There would hardly be enough paper to tell of all of the wonderful times we had together. The meetings were joyful and filled with laughter and fellowship. These dear folk loved to sing. We mainly sang hymns about Jesus. The ladies and gentlemen came to the class regularly. Some came to faith after just a few weeks. Others would attend for months or even years before receiving Jesus, Yeshua, as their Lord and Savior. It was a great joy to see many of these older people come to know the Lord and grow in their faith.

What We Believe

Every other month, I would write on the blackboard in large letters, "WHAT WE BELIEVE." I would then ask the older people, "Do you believe in Moses?" They would say, "Oh yes, yes." Then I, a Gentile person, would say, "So do I." Then I would make a check mark on the board indicating that the seniors believed in Moses and so did I. My next question was, "Do you believe in the prophets?" Once again they would say, "Yes." I said, "So do I," and again I would mark that on the board. Yet again, "Do you believe that God created the earth?" They would answer, "Oh yes, yes." On and on this would go, question after question, until there were about ten questions on the board. Finally I would ask, "Do you believe the Messiah is going to come?" After they agreed I would say, "So do I." By using these questions I had led them exactly where I wanted them to be. I would then direct them to look at all of the things that I had written on the board. I also pointed out and stressed the fact that they had agreed on every point. I would do this over and over again to drive home the point that Gentile believers believed in all of these things that Jewish people believe in. I then pointed out the only difference that Jewish people have with believers in Jesus. The difference is that believers in Jesus believe that the Messiah has already come one time and that He's going to come back a second time. I would then say, "That's the one big fact that we want to share with you. We would like you to know that the Messiah has come the first time to be the atonement for our sins. It was prophesied in your Scriptures (the Hebrew Scriptures or Old Testament) that He would come and do that for us." I then would finish up with a couple Messianic prophecies from the Old Testament Scriptures. This would reach people every time. I could just feel them following along with me.

It is interesting to note that the lesson worked very well but one wouldn't do that in the church. This was a group of mostly Jewish people. So, that was something that worked particularly well in a mission meeting. It also works well if you are witnessing to a Jewish friend.

Sue (Schwartz) Ciavolino Remembers

Rebecca Schwartz and Sue

Ruth and I go back to her time in California. I was born again in 1972. I was like a Jewish believing ink blotter. I read the Bible and everything that I could get my hands on about the Bible. In 1978, I moved out to California. This was when I met Ruth Wardell in person. We hit it off immediately. We loved each other's company. We used to meet on a regular basis. Ruth was teaching a Bible class for older Jewish men and women for ABMJ (CPM). She also hoped to lead these men and women to the Lord.

My mother, Rebecca, was not a believer. What was significant about my mother was that she was deaf and also blind in one eye. I used sign language to communicate with her. One day, I decided to take my mother to Ruth's class at the Center. My mother was a beautiful woman and very friendly. My mother sat with the other women facing Ruth, and I sat in a chair with my back to Ruth but facing my mother so that she could see me sign whatever Ruth would say.

Whenever I would sign, I would first say this prayer, "Lord, do not let the deaf person see me or my face. Let them see You and Your Word." As the class progressed, I could see that my mother was really enjoying the teaching. I could tell because, even though she was intently looking at my signing, she kept looking up at Ruth. Ruth told the group, "If any of you would like to receive Yeshua, your Messiah, as your savior, just raise your hand and we can pray together." My mother raised her hand. I blurted out loud, "There's a woman here raising her hand!" I did this to make sure that Ruth did not miss my mother's raised hand. Ruth said, "Oh, wonderful. Right after the meeting we will talk about this." Ruth ended the meeting with a prayer. She was speaking this prayer with her eyes closed. I was signing whatever Ruth was saying to my mother. My mother suddenly signed to me this question: "Is Ruth reading that prayer?" I signed, "No. No. The prayer is from Ruth's heart." My mother was amazed because Jewish people usually just read prayers from a prayer book.

When the meeting ended, Ruth came over and greeted us. We went to a couch area where we could sit and talk. Ruth asked my mother some questions and prayed with her to receive Jesus as her Lord. After my mother prayed, she opened her eyes and we talked. Some of the other unbelieving Jewish women there asked my mother some questions about what she had just done. I signed the questions for my mother and then answered as quickly and respectfully as I could. One little old lady walked over to my mother and said, "You don't want to do that. Jesus is not your God. You don't want to believe in Jesus. That's not for Jews." This woman was obviously an unbeliever, yet she was attending this Bible study class. My mother signed an answer, which I interpreted. My mother signed, "Oh, I feel 'safe.'" She used the sign that is specifically used for the word "salvation." It can also be used for "safe" but it is the sign used in churches for the word salvation. How could my mother possibly know to use that sign when she had just become a believer mere moments before? Ruth and I were shocked that my mother knew to use that particular sign for "salvation." We believe that it was the work of the Holy Spirit. I went out and bought her a large type Bible so that we could now read the Bible together. All throughout the years when I was with her, we would read the Bible. What a wonderful experience to see my dear mother come to know her Messiah!

Gentile believers can bring the new Jewish believer into the mission, but it is the mature Jewish believer who takes the new Jewish believer those final steps where they can have comfort that they are making the right decision to believe in Jesus. The Jewish person looks at a Gentile believer and figures that it is natural that they would believe in Jesus, but when they get in a room with all these older people who are Jewish believers, they feel more comfortable in making a profession of faith.

Satisfaction

Being in North Hollywood was somewhat different from when I was in New York. I remember these times as very happy times because of the many, many opportunities to witness to people who had just come into the Center off the street. The storefront was very effective since anyone who walked in came in because they were curious about what they had seen in the window or what they heard from somebody about this mission. It was much easier for a Jewish person to walk into this storefront than it was to have one of the workers speak to them in their very own homes. This was a very safe way for a Jewish person to investigate what this Center was doing. In the storefront, there was a reading room where anyone could sit down and read any of the tracts or books. If someone had questions, they

could ask one of the people there, or if they wanted to, they could pick themselves up and walk out. There was no threat at all.

Outside the building was a sign saying, "We believe in Moses, the Prophets, and Jesus the Messiah." This clearly identified the Center as a Messianic Center. People would come in, attracted by the sign, to find out exactly what it meant. The sign provoked Christians, Gentile believers, pastors, and other people to come in and get literature for their unbelieving Jewish neighbors and friends.

In the 1970s, many Jewish people came to faith in the North Hollywood Center. Sally Berent was just one of those people. She came in one day, spoke with people there, and eventually, she became a believer in Jesus. She became a very valuable worker for the mission as a volunteer.

The Large Sign

We had a large sign outside the North Hollywood Center. One important thing that I learned was that a mission center needs some kind of sign that says who you are in a plain way, even though some people had said that a sign for a Messianic ministry would turn Jewish people off. I objected and said, "No, it won't. It won't turn them off. It will turn them on. They will want to know why a place with a Jewish star believes in Jesus. It will provoke them to come into

the storefront to see. And surely if they're seeking, they will want to know the answer."

When I started working at the Center, there was a large cross inside of the Jewish star on the side of the building. I knew that this needed to be changed because the cross *would* turn away Jewish people. We were new to this neighborhood, and I knew that interacting with anyone that one does not know requires a lot of sensitivity if you wish to develop a good relationship. The cross has a special negative significance to a Jewish person. They learn from a very young age to avoid this symbol. When a Christian sees a cross, they see salvation. When a Jew sees a cross, they see a sword. This is a sword of death and destruction that is all too common in the history of Jews and Christians. I grabbed a ladder and climbed up almost twenty feet to paint over the cross so that it was not visible. Having a cross inside the star would make the neighborhood people irate. I said to one of my fellow workers at the mission, "How are you going to teach the people from the neighborhood the love of Jesus if you make them all upset?"

Sally Berent—Memories

I recall that one day I was led by the Holy Spirit to drive to North Hollywood to the Beth Sar Shalom Center where they were giving away a free calendar and a prophecy booklet. My older daughter was with me. My husband Larry and I had previously driven by the Center and had seen this big sign that said, "We believe in Moses, the Prophets, and Jesus the Messiah." At that time, the side of the building had a big Jewish Star with a cross in the middle. The Center was right in the middle of a large Jewish neighborhood. Larry and I are Jewish, and when I saw that sign, I exclaimed, "Oy gevalt!" This is a Yiddish expression of dismay. There was something that really bothered me about that sign. I just could not accept the Cross and the Jewish Star being displayed together.

Sometime later, I did go to Beth Sar Shalom for the Bible studies, which interested me greatly. This is how I met up with Ruth. I was in my thirties at that time, and I recall that there were a lot of older women in that class. I was so happy with these Bible study classes that I continued to attend and soon accepted Jesus as my Messiah. Not long after that, I began working for the mission in the office.

Sally Berent

Ruth never seemed to like paperwork. It just was not "her thing." Ruth would give me all of the necessary information and then tell me to complete the paperwork. I really liked speaking on the phone. Ruth gave me the nickname, "**M'MOC**" which stood for **M**otor **M**outh **O**ffice **C**onsultant. While we worked hard, there was always much to do. We loved to have fun. One Halloween, I found my car with tin cans tied all across the rear bumper. I was quite upset and this was quite apparent by the look on my face when I entered the Center. The minute I saw the look on Ruth's face I knew that she had done this. We all burst out laughing.

I was saved, but my husband Larry was not yet a believer. However, he used to come to all of the functions at the Center to help out in the kitchen or wherever assistance was needed. Ruth quickly made friends with Larry. There was one couple who worked at the Center. The woman was a Jewish believer, and her husband was a Gentile believer. They knew that Larry was not a believer, and whenever the opportunity presented itself, they would "shove" a Bible right in Larry's face. This bothered Larry greatly. Ruth asked them to please stop doing this. The woman's response was to explain that this was how she was saved, and she didn't understand why she couldn't speak to Larry in this manner. I patiently explained to her that while that might have been an effective method for her, it was extremely annoying to my husband. I explained that no matter how sincere her intentions were, one had to get to know a person before sharing the Gospel. Larry did not know these people, and he was quite annoyed by her aggressiveness. Another couple there went over to talk to Larry and thus saved him from this woman.

I asked Ruth why she had never witnessed to Larry, and she told me that she knew that I was witnessing to Larry. Ruth felt that she should just be his friend since I was doing the witnessing. Ruth believes that each person is unique, and one does not always have to be quoting chapter and verse to witness to someone. Larry eventually did receive the Lord, in Ruth's home, and he gave Ruth honor by saying that she was instrumental in his receiving the Lord. Larry came to faith in 1991 (during the Gulf War). Those times at the Center were Larry's happiest times. [*Editor's note*: Larry passed away in June of 2008.]

I was required to take the courses that they gave at Beth Sar Shalom about Judaism, doctrines, and witnessing to others. I was like many American Jewish people who had read little, if any, Scriptures. I learned a great deal about my Jewish heritage and the great truths of the Scriptures from these courses.

Margie Marder

Through the storefront ministry, many Jewish people who became believers found a family that they could relate to and grow in the Lord. One such person was Margie Marder. God in His mercy revealed to Margie that Jesus was the Jewish Messiah. She believed that she was the only Jewish person who believed in Him. She wrote the following story.

Margie Marder Writes

When I was thirty-five years old (I'm seventy now), I was married and had a two-year-old child. I had been brought up in a conservative and traditional Jewish family. I loved God and felt so happy and complete in the Jewish faith. I wasn't familiar with other faiths except Catholic because in our neighborhood we were all Jewish except for maybe three Italian families. Years later, my husband and I were married, and we moved from Brooklyn to California shortly thereafter.

About one year later, my husband and I went to see a new tax preparer in the San Fernando Valley. On the way home, we passed a storefront with a sign that said "Beth Sar Shalom…We believe in Moses, the Prophets, and Jesus the Messiah." We stopped and got the phone number. I was so excited when I called in the morning and spoke to Ruth Wardell. I told her about how God revealed Jesus to me and how I became a believer. The Center was having a luncheon that Friday, and Ruth asked me if I would like to attend. I excitedly waited for Friday to come. When I opened the door to Beth Sar Shalom, Ruth Wardell warmly greeted me, and I saw a room filled with mostly Jewish women, who along with my mentor Ruth Wardell became my new family. Ruth had many Bible teachings and musical gatherings for all of us. She was like a mother hen to baby chicks. This was the beginning of my walk with my Jewish Messiah.

Ruth Recalls Persecution and Vandalism in North Hollywood

Just a few doors down from the mission's storefront was an Orthodox Jewish bookstore called The House of David. I had developed a relationship with the owners, a father and son. I would often go and visit with the father and go out for coffee with the son to a nearby McDonald's. In the 1970s, we had to deal with neo-Nazis and the Ku Klux Klan. Both the Beth Sar Shalom storefront and the House of David Jewish bookstore were vandalized by these groups. The vandalism took the form of paint being splashed and sprayed on the front of these stores as well as plate glass windows being broken. This happened a few times. Many times,

swastikas were painted on the front of both storefronts, and I would paint over these hateful, offensive symbols. It's interesting to note that Jews and Jewish believing organizations received the same treatment from these groups. They even put a bomb under the car of the owner of the bookstore one time. They were really after him. They didn't like Jews. This was a Jewish neighborhood. In their ignorance, they couldn't tell the difference between a Jewish bookstore and a Messianic Jewish Center. They both had Jewish items in the windows of their storefronts.

There were a lot of bomb scares. The usual procedure would be that the police would receive a call with the bomb threat, and they would then relate that to me so that I could take appropriate action. They were pretty wild times, but the mission grew and people continued to get saved, and more and more people were coming into the Center.

Someone had called and said that they were going to bomb the Center. We couldn't tell everybody that we had a bomb threat, so we held our meetings anyway. We figured that God would take care of us. One time, after we had received one of these calls, I was playing the piano. The kitchen was right behind the wall where the piano was located. A lady by the name of Barbara Benedict was singing a solo. When she came to the last note of the song, there was a loud bang from behind the wall in the kitchen. I thought to myself that they are bombing us now. I quickly ran back to see what had happened. Apparently some pans had fallen on the floor in the kitchen. I breathed a sigh of relief.

On another occasion, the police had informed the workers at the mission that the threat they had received indicated that a bomb would go off sometime between two and four early in the morning one day that week. The policemen said that somebody needed to be there to protect the building. I asked myself, "Who is going to sit in this building?" I called Maddy, a Jewish believer who worked for the mission. I told her that someone had to be at the building between two and four in the middle of the night as the police had suggested. I said to Maddy,

"If you come one night, I'll come another." Maddy was shaking in her boots at the thought of sitting there while someone might be coming to toss a bomb into the mission. Ultimately, neither one of us went to sit in the mission in the middle of the night. The mission had an alarm system installed, and the police suggested that perhaps I could watch from across the street. In the end, the place was never bombed. Praise the Lord!

At one point in time, it was the Jewish Defense League that was coming against Chosen People Ministries and the work they were doing at the Center. The Jewish Defense League is a radical pro-Jewish group known for protecting Jews from any form of anti-Semitism. They would come in the middle of the night and break the windows of the mission. After breaking the windows, they would enter the mission and throw over the bookcases and the display cases that held all of the publications that the mission had for the people. Jewish missions love the Jewish people, but the Jewish Defense League saw our work as somehow being anti-Semitic. Finally, Dr. Daniel Goldberg, who was the director of the North Hollywood region of ABMJ, got on their case, and they stopped doing that kind of activity.

I remember one time when I was driving to a funeral. I lived not far from the mission, so my route took me past the Center. As I drove past, I was shocked to see over 200 holes that had been shot into the doors and windows of the mission. One window was completely out, and as a result I could not attend the funeral because I could not leave the mission without any supervision, as people might come in and just do more damage.

I worked in the mission from 1973 until 1985, a period of twelve years, and this type of vandalism went on for quite a few years. Every day before I went home, I would circle the mission, just to make sure that all the windows were in place and not damaged. There was quite a bit of persecution for the mission in those times.

One time, the town asked if they could use the Center for a voting place. I gave them permission. On Election Day, they required that we cover up all of our literature materials, as is required in a voting place. Jewish people, however, knew who we were, and they would not come into the place to vote, so they had to take the voting booth out onto the street. That was the only year that I agreed to do that.

The entire neighborhood in North Hollywood changed over the period of twelve to fifteen years that I spent in the mission. The most important change was that the Jewish population moved out. This movement out of the neighborhood started around the time that I came in 1973 but had reached the level at which there were very few Jewish people left in the neighborhood by 1985. The Jewish bookstore, the Jewish bakery and other Jewish businesses in the neighborhood closed and moved on. This bakery had great food, but when the people left, the bakery left, and the food left.

Despite the many times that the windows were broken and the bomb threats, etc., God in His mercy kept us all safe and a great many Jewish people accepted the Lord through the work done in these two storefronts. Praise the Lord!

The HAG Society

There was a club in the North Hollywood Center for the older people called the HAG Society. The acronym HAG meant "Hardening of the Arteries Girls" or "Hardening of the Arteries Gentlemen." Lil Highbloom, one of the members, was the president of the club. The club was given this name because everybody there was always forgetting something. I would tell the people to join up but to make sure they didn't forget to pay their dues. Of course everyone forgot to pay their dues. I would then inform the group that Lil Highbloom was the president of the club, but that Lil would probably forget, so when they saw Lil they should remind her that she's the president of the club. We all enjoyed the *kibbitzing* that the HAG

Society brought to us. [*Editor's note*: *kibbitz* is Yiddish for "to chat, to gossip, to make small talk or idle chatter."]

Field Trips with the Seniors

I used to take groups on many outings. I would also take the older people on "trips to Israel" which were actually in the hills near North Hollywood. I would make a list of things that people should bring on a trip to Israel. Then I would charge them three dollars round-trip for the transportation. One day, a man called me on the phone asking about this trip. I told him that the cost would be three dollars round-trip. He said to me, "Did you say $3,000?" I said, "No, I said three dollars." This man did not understand how a trip halfway around the world to Israel could cost so little. What I did not explain to him was that these trips took place right in California. I would take the group up into the hills near a lake, and they would make believe that they were at sites in Israel such as the Sea of Galilee, the Mount of Olives, etc. California is very similar to Israel in many ways. They have similar weather and rain patterns. It is easy to find places in California that look a lot like places in Israel.

One time, twenty-five of us went on a field trip up the coast of California. I had a van in which I could fit fourteen or fifteen people, and then there were a couple of cars following behind. A lot of witnessing took place on these outings. This type of situation allows for one-on-one witnessing. New ladies to the mission would come on these trips because they were drawn by the love of the group.

Usually when you get older people together, they argue and fight and fuss. There are all kinds of "I don't like you" type stuff that goes on. This group didn't have any of that. They had fun, and there was much laughter. They had happy times, and this is what drew the people to these activities. It was a very contagious kind of happiness. These older people would participate in the trips, and little by little, they would come to believe in Jesus. One woman took thirteen years to come to believe in Jesus, but she did believe.

Jean Ambro

Jean Ambro was a part-time worker in the North Hollywood Mission. She has a great love for the Jewish people. We would do a lot of street work and home visitations. She would drive all over the place to bring Jewish people to the Center. She was an energetic worker for Christ and, today, at the age of ninety-one (June of 2009), she still teaches classes and rejoices about the Jews who are listening to the Good News about their Messiah. She holds these Bible classes today in senior citizens' homes.

We worked in the North Hollywood Center together where she taught the children's classes with me. She loved children, which was an asset since we would hold these classes in a small room (fifteen feet by fifteen feet) with maybe fifteen to twenty children in there at one time. The children never got up and ran around, as this was against the rules that we had established. They had to stay in the room until a parent came to pick them up. This was never a problem for us. We would have the best times. In fact, the children could not wait until the next class. The room would always be full. We played games and taught the lessons and learned Bible verses.

Jean was very faithful. She was always on time and always there to serve the Lord. She was used of the Lord to lead Richard Cohn to salvation. At one time, Richard was one of our missionaries in North Hollywood and led the Los Angeles division of CPM. Jean Ambro was the evangelist of the evangelists for Jewish people. She had the gift of evangelism as well as teaching. She was just able to bring them in. When Jean worked in the Center, there was hardly a day that someone did not come in off the street that Jean would witness to. Jean loved to do that. She was a very valuable worker at the Center.

Jean Ambro Remembers (at Ninety-One Years of Age)

I had heard about the ministry that Ruth was doing with Jewish people and began to bring people I knew to her Bible class. Shortly thereafter, I began working for Ruth. We became acquainted, and I spent fifteen years at the North Hollywood Center on Victory Boulevard.

Jean Ambro

Sometimes, I helped out when Ruth would have the children bring sleeping bags to stay overnight in the mission. Ruth and I would lead the Jewish children in studying the Word of God and singing songs. When the children would fall asleep, Ruth would color their faces with water-based magic markers. When they woke up the following morning, they would point at each other and laugh loudly, not realizing that they all had had their faces painted. The children really enjoyed these overnights.

We would take the older people on trips to a large hotel and retreat center called Arrowhead Springs up in the mountains. We had marvelous times with them there and would hear great speakers. They loved to go on these trips. Some people who would not attend the Bible class had no problem going on these trips. In fact, they loved doing almost anything that Ruth planned for them.

Mother Rose

Mother Rose and Ruth

Mother Rose was a Jewish woman who did not want to believe in Jesus. She came from a very Orthodox Jewish background. Rose had been brought to the Center by some friends, yet she was very angry. She really didn't want to be there. As a result, when she attended the mission, she sat in the back. It took a long time before this changed. She began to move a little bit closer to the front each time she came. Eventually, she not only became a believer in Jesus, but she would witness to every person that she met. She had progressed from not wanting to be at the mission at all to becoming an evangelist for the Lord. Once, she saw a rabbi get on a bus. She went and sat next to him so that she could share the good news of Jesus with him. She even went to the store and bought some food just so that she could bring people in off the street and feed hungry people in her home while she shared the Gospel message with them.

The Ninety-Year-Old Jewish Man: Mr. Mitchnick

Mr. Mitchnik

There was a ninety-year-old Jewish man, Mr. Mitchnick, who had experienced and survived a pogrom when he was a child in Russia. A pogrom is an organized massacre of helpless people. This pogrom was carried out by soldiers who were part of the Russian Orthodox Church. As a child, he'd been knocked unconscious and thrown on a cart filled with the dead, naked bodies of Jewish people. He appeared to be dead. All of a sudden, he moved, and a woman saw him. This woman dragged him off the cart and took him to her home, saving his life. He made his way to the United States and eventually opened an accordion shop in California. He played the accordion beautifully.

Mr. Mitchnick would come to the mission. The only reason he came was because he married a woman, Rose, who brought him along. Rose, who was a Gentile, became a believer and became a great witness for Jesus. In fact, she was the one who brought Mother Rose to the mission. If I mentioned the name of Jesus, he would just *plotz* (Yiddish for "to be aggravated beyond one's patience"). He would loudly object to us when we would say the name of Jesus. This was the reaction that he had to Christians because of the persecution in Russia. Rose said that she would do anything and endure anything, if only her husband would become a believer. When Rose got cancer the first time, she witnessed to her husband, but that did not convince him. However, the second time she went through this, he became a believer when he was ninety-two years old.

I remember that when I got cancer, Mr. Mitchnick came and stood at the end of the bed and said he was going to pray for me in Jesus' name and that he knew in his heart that I was going to get better. I remember how difficult it was putting up with this man before he became a believer because of all the things that he spouted at the mission. However, here he stood praying for me in the name of Jesus. Eventually, he was baptized. That was a great day! God works often beyond what we could ask or think. Praise the Lord!

Ruth's Memories of Lil Highbloom

Lil Highbloom was a Jewish believer from a very Orthodox Jewish background. The first time I met Lil was on a visitation call. The mission office had given me her name. She lived in a one-bedroom apartment on the second floor. Her husband Ralph lived most of the time at the Veteran's Hospital. He had a multitude of medical problems from being in combat in World War II. He was also emotionally unstable as a result of his experiences in the war. Lil had come to California from Cleveland.

Ruth and Lil Highbloom

She was led to the Lord by a missionary there who had brought her to faith in her Messiah Jesus and discipled her.

When I first chatted with Lil, she was quite discouraged, and her faith was not strong. Life had been difficult for her because of the move from Cleveland to California. She also was disheartened by the condition of her husband. I invited Lil to a meeting, and Lil responded angrily, saying, "Who wants to come to your meeting? I'm not coming!" She asked many questions, but I noticed that as our conversation progressed, she had softened somewhat. She eventually told me that she would come to the meeting.

She was so pleased with that first meeting that she attended the meetings regularly, never missing one. She was one of the best students of the Word of God in the class. Each meeting increased her trust in the Lord. We became good friends, and I had the joy of sharing many things with her. She never missed an opportunity to share Jesus with Jewish people.

One time, Lil became ill and had to be hospitalized. I set out to visit with her to bring some comfort and to encourage her in her time of need. As I entered her hospital room, she greeted me with these words: "I prayed for you this morning."

"So, what did you pray?" I asked. I never expected the answer that I received.

Lil said, "I prayed that if you had any pain in your back or if you had a headache, that the Lord should give me your pain and I would bear it so that you would be free to share Jesus with other Jewish people."

I didn't suffer from back pain or headaches, but this amazed me. No one had ever prayed that prayer for me before. In fact, I could not remember that I had ever prayed that prayer for anyone else. I thanked her for her prayer, and as was her custom, she repeated the prayer. By the time she finished praying, we both had tears in our eyes. I was overwhelmed that Lil was willing to suffer for me. Immediately, I was reminded of Jesus and His great love in bearing my sins for me. Then I prayed that if ever the occasion arose in my life, God would give me the grace to be willing, as Lil was, to bear someone else's burden so that they might be free to do their work.

Lil's Answered Prayer

One Sunday, I went to pick up Lil to take her for a ride. She was extremely nervous. Her husband, Ralph, was home for the weekend from the Veteran's Hospital. He was quite agitated and upset. He told Lil that he didn't want to go back to the hospital. She then told me that he had been brandishing a knife and threatening her.

Lil got into the car, and as I pulled away from her house, I said to her, "Lil, the Lord will do something. When you get home, Ralph will be willing to go back to the hospital." Lil looked at me nervously and said, "What can happen? We won't be gone very long." She didn't sound too confident. I decided to drive to the country for lunch. As we drove along, we chatted, and I could still sense her concern, although she did relax a little.

When we pulled into the driveway at her home, we did not know what to expect. Lil anxiously opened the front door, and there was Ralph quietly awaiting our return. While we were away, he had developed a fever. He was anxious to get back to the hospital where he would receive medication to relieve it. While he was awaiting our return, he had figured out the quickest route to the hospital. Lillian couldn't believe what she had seen or heard. Both of us thanked God for His answer to her need. God hears and answers prayer. Praise the Lord!

Gladys

One of the special people who came to classes in North Hollywood was Gladys. Gladys was a very Jewish person. She had one son who was living a Jewish Orthodox lifestyle and another son who was a believer in Jesus, whom I saw occasionally. Gladys eventually became a believer. She had a very simple way of looking at things. One time, we were in the car, and Gladys told me about some disappointment in her life. I said to her, "Why don't you pray to Jesus about that disappointment, and He will take it away." Gladys prayed right there and then in the car while we were driving. Gladys turned to me and said, "Well, it's all gone now. I won't feel bitter or disappointed anymore." This is a good example of the simple faith that Gladys had in Jesus. I can't remember her being disappointed after this.

Her one son, who practiced Orthodox Judaism, was unaware that his mother was a believer. At the mission one day, for some reason, I moved the curtain back in the window, and there was her son standing outside on the street looking in the window. The son knew me because he had previously met me when I was with his mother, but he didn't know who I was or that I worked at this Jewish Christian mission. Well, when he saw me inside this mission, he realized exactly what was going on, and he came inside the storefront ranting and raving. He threatened to ruin the mission and even to blow it up. For half an hour, he went on and on and on, venting at me. I found out that soon after this encounter, he abandoned Orthodox Judaism because there was no meaning to it in his life. I don't know whatever happened to him, but I do know that his mother, Gladys, did accept the Lord.

I couldn't help but love Gladys. I learned a great deal through being with her. She had a simple faith in Jesus, which I did not see often in life. She often blessed me more than I blessed her.

CHAPTER 14
Classes for Younger Women

I also had a group of younger women who were in their late thirties, forties, and fifties who would come to class. They came every week and never missed. They would bring their friends, and the class grew in size. It was a great time of learning, and there was a lot of witnessing that went on.

If you speak to those women now, they would tell you that this class was a highlight of their lives. I still keep in touch with many of these people, so I am very aware of the influence that those days of ministry had on them. They grew in the Word and really seemed to be blessed. This was a very satisfying time for me and for these people. We would have women's meetings there and fill up the hall with seventy to seventy-five women, most of them Jewish. They would come from all over the hills in West Los Angeles and other places in Orange County.

The mission also attended to people's social needs and often had a couple's club which worked very, very well. All of these classes and clubs were greatly used of the Lord to share Jesus as the Messiah. Many became believers.

Jackie Chernak—Memories

My family and I are Jewish. We came to California from England in September of 1960. There were six of us in all. In 1961, we all accepted Jesus as our Jewish Messiah. We also became staunch members of Beth Sar Shalom which was part of ABMJ. The mission became our home away from home. Its leaders and staff workers became our friends and family. It was about 1974 when a never-to-be-forgotten figure arrived in our lives in the person of Ruth Wardell.

Jackie Chernak and Ruth

At first, this tall, imposing lady, seemingly so straight-laced and proper, was just another Bible teacher that we would have to get used to. We met on a more personal basis when my mother and I took food to Gladys, one of the ladies who attended classes at the mission (see p. 140). Ruth was already there doing what was to become known to me through the years as

"Ruth giving of Ruth and her Lord." She began the visit with us by trying on wigs and making us laugh. We began to realize that this was no "straight-laced, proper missionary Bible teacher" type. This was the unique Ruth Wardell.

In our Tuesday Bible classes in the North Hollywood Center, Ruth made the Bible come bouncing to life with interesting facts. Jesus was right there in the classroom with us. Heaven and the Rapture had always been a bit scary to me. However, now they were a wonder and a joy that awaited me. We grew in the Lord and became involved in other people's lives. Ruth knew how to bring together a mixed group of women, from different backgrounds, types, and ages, and make them into a cohesive group. We loved the Lord and cared about each other.

We watched Ruth go through cancer and surgery. A group of us went to the hospital and trailed the gurney as the medical personnel guided it through the hospital hallways, until they arrived at the operating room and we could follow it no further. Ruth was singing songs and praising the Lord until the sedative made her so sleepy that she could not sing anymore. She came through the surgery just fine and recovered well.

She has been my mentor in so many ways. I've learned more about my Jewishness from Ruth, who, though a Gentile Christian, has herself learned and knows more about Jewish people, their laws and customs than I will ever know.

Ruth wanted the church people to hear and understand why Jews didn't easily accept the Lord—and to teach them how to reach out in love. So we role-modeled before the church assembly. She was the interviewer, and I was the Jewish person, explaining the Jewish point of view. This gave many non-Jewish believers a far better understanding and perspective of the Jewish mindset. Many came up to us and applauded our method of teaching them something so important. They left us with the promise that they could now more sensitively witness to their Jewish friends, and even tell Gentile Christians, family, and friends of their newly acquired knowledge. It was indeed heartening to be part of such a wonderful accomplishment.

Deborah (Schmidtt) Kenna—Memories

(Sister of Susan Barr and Melissa Barr)

I feel very blessed to have met Ruth Wardell. She taught me so much about my Jewish heritage. She also helped me to understand more about Judaism. I had been a believer but did not understand everything. I grew up not knowing much about Judaism, as my family was one of the few Jewish families that did not really teach me about my heritage.

I became a believer in 1981 when I moved to California. Ruth was very instrumental in my coming to faith. She taught me about how Jesus is the Messiah. I then started to study with her, and it all began to make sense. I told my two sisters that I had accepted the Lord into my life, and they thought that I had joined a cult. A short time after that, my younger sister, Melissa, decided to go to a Christian retreat directed by none other than Ruth Wardell. While she was

Deborah, Melissa, Susan

on that retreat, Melissa accepted the Lord. My older sister, Susan, studied the Bible, and she too came to faith. Soon, we all grew very close to Ruth, a wonderful, loving compassionate lady who became a very dear friend.

Melissa Barr Campbell—Memories

It was about twenty years ago when I was in my twenties. I was becoming more and more disillusioned with life and what my purpose in life was. I had always believed in God and was always a seeker of truth. Born Jewish, my parents did not raise my sisters and me in the religion to any great extent. Our family celebrated a conglomeration of holidays—Christmas without a tree, Easter with eggs and rabbits, Jewish High Holidays and Passover only when we were around the relatives. Needless to say, we were confused. Yet, years later, a loving, kind, and faithful woman came along to share a great truth which ultimately led to our freedom.

I was working in a small business in Burbank, California. Also working there was a lovely girl who was a friend of my sister Debbie. This girl, who was a born-again believer in Jesus, invited us to a conference of women. We knew it would be a "religious" conference and didn't know what to expect. There was a speaker there named Ruth Wardell. We were told that she was a missionary to the Jews. We didn't have a clue as to what that meant! Isn't it funny that of the 300 women at the conference, my sister and I (and one other woman who was a friend of Ruth's) were the only Jewish people there! Ruth's words were exceptional. She was so confident in her speaking that you knew immediately that she believed what she was saying beyond a shadow of a doubt. As she spoke, it was apparent that she had a real love for God and that love overflowed to the audience.

This speech was unlike anything I had ever heard. She spoke about Jesus being a Jew and the promised Messiah. She told us why the Jewish people had such a hard time coming to Him. She talked about the Bible and prophecies. I was transfixed as I listened. Deep in my spirit, something said she was right. It was then that I came to see Jesus in the context of Christmas, yet I also knew that I was Jewish and I wasn't supposed to believe in Him. As I listened to the words that Ruth spoke, I became confused and scared. Everything in my being wanted to run to her because I needed to have her explain it all to me. I needed Ruth Wardell to help me understand the facts that were confusing me. It was at that conference that we were blessed with a woman whose sole purpose was to reach out to the Jews to share the Messiah's love. Speaking with Ruth about Jesus was life-changing. A window that was locked shut my whole life was now opening, allowing the Spirit of God to blow through and begin to move in my heart and my life.

Ruth took my sisters and me under her wing. It wasn't long before I accepted the Lord as my Savior at a Bible church that Ruth attended. My sister and I "went forward" together. After we came to faith, Ruth discipled us from a Jewish perspective. We learned the basics from one of the best. She introduced my sister Debbie and me to wonderful Jewish believers, including Arnold Fruchtenbaum and Louis Lapides who, along with her, laid the foundation through their teachings for a strong walk with God. Not long after, my other sister, Susan, came to the Lord. We spent many hours with Ruth in discipleship classes, Bible studies, and fellowship over a period of several years. As a result of Ruth's teaching and nurturing, it was one of the most rewarding periods of my life.

I say with fervor that Ruth Wardell is a wonderful, faithful woman—an angel, in fact. I am sure there is a huge smile on God's face as she submits over and over again to His Will. She shared His goodness with my sisters and me because she cared.

My Years at the North Hollywood Center

Working in the North Hollywood Center was a great experience for me as a missionary. I found my years at the North Hollywood Mission very exciting, happy, and productive. As I write this, I realize how God put this Center into my life and gave me the joy of knowing that, over the years, the Gospel was shared with multitudes of people. God also blessed me by my seeing so many Jewish people come to know their Messiah.

There were new Jewish people to witness to all the time coming in off the streets, and the meetings were filled predominantly with Jewish believers and always a few unbelievers. We often celebrated "special occasions" with over seventy-five people attending. Eighty-five percent of those people were Jewish. They learned much from the hymns. They didn't need a reinforcement of their Jewish identity. Most of these people were from Orthodox or Conservative Jewish backgrounds, and they knew that they were Jews and what it meant to be Jewish. They fell in love with Jesus, and so I sang hymns when they attended. Many of the older people became believers in Jesus. The meetings were a team effort by Jean Ambro, Rose Mitchnick, Madeline Goldberg, and me. We were four Gentile women who were sharing the Good News of Jesus with these Jewish men and women. Teams are a wonderful way to have success in ministry. I very much loved working with these ladies.

CHAPTER 15
Workers

Madeline Goldberg, Wife of Dr. Daniel Goldberg, Remembers

Daniel and Madeline Goldberg

I am delighted to share some of my experiences with Ruth, as I was privileged to work closely with her in behalf of Jewish evangelism, especially in teaching Bible classes and in holding special services in observance of Jewish holidays. I have observed with much joy the success of Ruth's ministry, a success and fruitfulness that speaks for itself—with many Jewish women coming to saving faith in Messiah Jesus. This is due, of course, to Ruth's unswerving devotion to the Lord and her faithfulness in serving Him continually up to this present hour.

Donna Jean Wood Remembers

I've known Ruth Wardell since 1972. My husband George and I had the privilege of serving the Lord together through Chosen People Ministries. I am a Hebrew-Christian. Ruth would often be the speaker for many Hebrew-Christian conferences, and I would give my testimony. George and I also occasionally provided the music at these meetings. I even sang at Ruth's retirement dinner in 1986.

Some years ago, I was very ill. This was at the time that Ruth was living in California, about a forty-minute drive from us. She called me on the phone one day and said to me, "Donna Jean, I'm going to devote my time to you until we get you well." She would come over every week which was quite a drive. Each week she would bring many copies of one Bible verse. She would post those

Don Wardell, Donna Jean Wood, and Ruth—at Ruth's 40th Anniversary with CPM

copies of the Bible verse all over my house so that I could learn that verse by memory. She would bring a different verse each week. Ruth also faithfully took me to the doctor's office. This went on for several months, and by the grace of God, good medical care, the prayers of Ruth, and the Word of God that Ruth shared with me, I was healed. I still have a lot of those Bible verses tucked away. They mean a great deal to me. Ruth became like a sister and a mentor to me. The best way to describe Ruth Wardell would be compassionate, unselfish, and always willing to share the Lord's Word.

Edith and Bill Freeman

I worked with Edith and Bill Freeman most of the years that I was in California (1973 – 1993). Edith Freeman came from an Orthodox Jewish background. She was a very vivacious witness to people. Both Edith and her husband were great witnesses for the Lord. Wherever they went, they were always sharing the Gospel. Both of them were a real expression of how one should do missionary work. Edith taught Bible classes. She was a good teacher and very Jewish in her approach.

Edith and Bill Freeman

Edith Freeman—Memories

In the early 1970s, Richard Cohn, who was in charge of the Chosen People Ministries mission in Los Angeles, had heard about my interest in Jewish evangelism. He called me and asked if I was interested in working for the mission. Bill and I agreed and went to California. That is where we met Ruth Wardell. Ruth was in charge of the mission, which was in a storefront in the San Fernando Valley. We were asked to train with her. I didn't feel that I needed any Jewish training, but my husband Bill did. The training was very helpful. Ruth was especially good with the children, and she had a real calling on her life for children's ministry.

Ruth was and is a very organized woman. She knew exactly what she wanted to accomplish in the mission. Our holiday meetings were the most tremendous events. We had large numbers of people at our Passover celebrations, as was the case with all of the Feasts of the Lord.

Ruth also led a Bible Study. We worked with her, and she worked with mostly Orthodox Jewish seniors. The way she taught them made for a fantastic ministry. The amazing thing was that these Orthodox people sat and listened to every word Ruth had to say. She never put any pressure on these people to accept Jesus. All she did was to teach them the Word of God.

We would speak to most of these people, but they really didn't want to speak about Jesus to anyone else but Ruth.

Ruth was a missionary, but Bill and I were evangelists. We got right to the point, which really did not work in the setting that Ruth had at that storefront mission. I worked with Ruth for fifteen years. I'm different than she is. Ruth is very gentle. I'm a Jew who wants to get the Word across to other people. I'm also from New York. In New York, we don't play games. We tell it like it is. Just like Ruth, I'm still out there sharing the Word. I'm seventy-nine and still going strong.

Dr. Vera Schlamm

[*Editor's note*: Vera Schlamm was born into a Jewish family on February 28, 1923, in Berlin, Germany. When she was fifteen, the family fled the Nazi persecution in Germany and traveled to Amsterdam in Holland. In 1943, at the age of twenty, Vera and her family were taken by the Germans and put into a concentration camp in Holland. Just before her 21st birthday, the Germans moved the family to Bergen-Belsen concentration camp in northwestern Germany. After the war, Vera and her family made their way to the United States, where she became a pediatrician. In July of 1960, Vera received Jesus as her Messiah. She became a great witness to her Jewish brothers and sisters.]

Ruth and Vera Schlamm

Vera Schlamm and I have been very good friends for over thirty years. She was a victim and survivor of the Nazi Holocaust in Europe. She was in the camps when she was in her middle teens during World War II. I always found it challenging to be with her because of her conversations about life in the camps and what she had witnessed and endured. These conversations were always turned into a blessing as Vera would share the many times that God answered her prayers and brought her through many hardships and difficulties.

I met Vera in 1970 at a conference trip sponsored by Fellowship of Christian Testimonies to the Jews (FCTJ) in upstate New York, where many missions and missionaries met together. I got to know Vera at that conference when I drove her to the airport. We spent some time together there and became acquainted. When I moved to California in 1973, I got in touch with her, and for the time that I was there, spent a great deal of time with her.

Vera is one of the most wonderful Christians that you could meet. At the present time (2008), she is experiencing many health problems, but her joy in the Lord is very strong. She loves to study the Bible and spends a lot of time listening to tapes on the Word of God from her pastor. She has been used of the Lord to bring many to know Jesus.

One time, Vera, her mother (whom Vera called "Muti"), Vera's pastor (who had led her to the Lord), and I were visiting together. Muti said, "There are three types of people in this room." She began with Vera and the minister and said that they were Christians. She would not admit in the least that Vera was Jewish. She then said that she was Jewish. Finally, she came to me. She said, "And then there's Ruth. She is half Jewish and half Christian." Vera's mother could not understand how I could know all about Jewish things, since I was not Jewish to begin with.

Vera and I still maintain our friendship to this day. I went to visit her for Christmas of 2007 and had the joy to fellowship with her one more time.

Dr. Vera Schlamm—Memories

Vera and her mother "Muti"

Ruth and I ministered together a lot for Chosen People Ministries in California. I met her in New York when I spoke at a meeting. This was just before she moved out to California in 1973. After that, we became friends. We ministered together, mostly in the Fresno area of California. We would visit many churches during the Jewish holidays, especially Passover. When we started ministering about these holidays, I learned a lot from Ruth, and then eventually I would go out by myself to teach about the Jewish holidays. I am Jewish and grew up with all of these holidays, but there was so much that I did not know until Ruth taught me. I knew about the traditional Jewish celebrations, but Ruth was able to teach me about the Messianic significance of things, such as the four cups of wine during the Passover Seder meal, which I had never learned from any Jewish person.

My mother lived with me for the last six and a half years of her life. Ruth helped a lot with drawing her to the Lord. Eventually, at the age of eighty-six, my mother did come to know the Lord. In many ways, the Lord helped me to minister to my mother, who only lived for about four months after accepting the Lord. I called my mother "Muti." This is a German term of endearment for "Mom." When Ruth took my mother on outings in her van, she would call my mother "Queen Muti" because in this van she sat very high up as though she were on a throne. My mother loved when Ruth would do that.

Senior Retreat

In the church that I attended from 1978 to 1986, we had what was called "Shalom Fellowship." We had monthly meetings in different homes. This meeting had a dual purpose. One purpose was to reach unsaved Jewish people. Jewish believers could bring their unsaved Jewish friends to this gathering. The fact that this was in a house and not in a church was non-threatening to the unsaved Jewish person. Ruth would bring a group of people from the Valley. Some of them were believers, and they enjoyed the meetings very much. We would usually have a speaker and nice Jewish music. The second purpose was to teach Gentiles how to witness to Jewish people. Interestingly, almost from the beginning, my mother always would attend these meetings. At first, she acted as though she were doing me a big favor. Shortly thereafter, when I would tell her that Friday night was the next Shalom Fellowship, she would quickly call for an appointment with her hair stylist. She really enjoyed coming to these meetings.

I don't believe that people have to be theology scholars to be saved. That's not what the Bible says. All one has to do to be saved is to believe in Jesus. I often think of the people who went into the gas chambers during the Holocaust. I saw a short video at the Holocaust Museum in Washington, D.C., where many went into the gas chambers saying, "*Ani ma'meem*," which means "I believe." I believe that if they sincerely believed in their hearts, the Lord somehow revealed Himself to them at the last moment. In some way, He's going to be gracious to them. We cannot know who is saved or not. We can never put anybody in heaven or hell. That is between God and the individual.

Through Ruth, Chosen People Ministries arranged senior retreats for Jewish people, saved or unsaved. One year, the theme was "Growing Older Gracefully and Growing Older Gratefully." That theme stuck in my mind, and I just informed my Pastor that if I get to a point where I do not exhibit growing older gracefully and gratefully, then he should let me know.

Having survived the Nazi concentration camps took a toll on me physically. Damage to my liver and leaky heart valves caused by the brutal treatment by the Nazis took its toll on my stamina. As I have grown older, I have slowed down even more.

I have been to the Holocaust Museum in Washington, D.C., and Yad Vashem, the Holocaust Museum in Israel. [*Editor's note*: The name of the museum, *Yad Vashem*, is taken from Isaiah 56:5, "And to them will I give in my house and within my walls *a memorial and a name* (*Yad Vashem*) that shall not be cut off."] Both times that I visited Yad Vashem, I asked myself, "Why am I here?" I really can't take it. The last time, I walked in—and walked right through and back out again. It's just too hard for me. As for the Holocaust Museum in Washington, I went because I wanted to see what they had done. I gave money and supported it because I believe that it is important for people to remember what happened. It is very well done. In some ways, it is better than Yad Vashem in that when you first walk in you feel the oppression of the concentration camps. When I walked in, I experienced a great oppression. I saw the watch towers and experienced the emotions from that time in my life. When I went there, I tried to concentrate on other things like the boats that the Danish people used to smuggle people out of Nazi-occupied territories. I tried to focus on anything the least bit positive. I had three Gentile people with me, and I felt that it was good for them to see this so that they would understand better about what had happened there. If it hadn't been for that, I probably would have walked out. It is also important for Jewish people to see what their families and ancestors went through.

[*Editor's note*: Dr. Vera J. Schlamm went home to be with the Lord on November 3, 2008. She was eighty-five years old.]

Elena Parker - Memories

Ruth and Elena Parker

I was a fairly young believer when I first met Ruth Wardell at the North Hollywood branch of Chosen People Ministries, Beth Sar Shalom. She has had such an amazing impact on my life! Her love for my Jewish people is so special! When I was a new believer of two years or so, her life encouraged me to grow in the Lord. Later, the Lord used her to influence my mom into the kingdom. Ruth had plans to go on vacation to Northern California. It was 8 p.m., and she hadn't even packed her bags. However, she remembered her promise to me. She had promised to visit my mom who had cancer and did not have long to live. Ruth was driving home to finish packing when the Lord caused her to turn her car around to go visit my mom. She had only been to my home a few times, but the Lord showed Ruth the way there!

Later, Ruth told me that my mom received her with much joy and even took out a Bible. None of us had ever seen my mother with a Bible before. Ruth told me that my mom opened to Isaiah 53. Ruth saw that there was a big red circle around that chapter. My mom asked

Ruth to explain why it was that the Jewish Bible spoke so clearly about Jesus. That night, with Ruth at her side, my mom confessed Jesus as her very own Messiah.

Ruth left for her vacation the next day, and my mom lost her voice due to the cancer in her throat. One week later, my mother was scheduled for surgery to remove this tumor. Fifteen minutes before her surgery, the Lord prompted me to ask her if she had believed in Jesus. Since she could not talk, she only nodded indicating, "Yes." She did believe in Jesus. Before the surgery could take place, the tumor broke loose and suffocated her. It wasn't until Ruth returned from her trip that she told me about my mom's new-found faith that had happened the previous week! The Lord is faithful, and He uses faithful servants such as "Ruth with the Truth!"

P.S. I always tell Ruth that when the Lord takes her home that I should be so fortunate as to have just one-tenth of her spirit!

Jerry Gross Remembers

My relationship with Ruth goes back to the days when I was a missionary with Chosen People Ministries in the early 1980s. I had heard of Ruth Wardell, but I had never met her. I did know that she was legendary in the history of the mission. What really impressed me was that here was someone who was *not* Jewish having a special calling upon her life that not only drove her to be an effective evangelist to the Jewish people but also to be a leader and a pioneer in the Messianic Jewish movement. She was an example for many others who followed.

The thing that always amazed me was that Ruth always had fresh ideas. She wasn't locked into the "old" ways of doing things. She has always stayed "young." Even when the new, younger workers were coming into the mission and making changes, Ruth was flexible enough to grow and embrace the "new" things. She was able to help in the building of Messianic Congregations. In her early years, there were virtually no Messianic Congregations.

The most important thing that I can say about Ruth is that she is such a godly example. She has been consistent in a movement that has had so many people come and go and not really make a difference. She, however, has been faithful.

Ruth's Ministry in Churches—Speaking in Ladies' Classes

Beth Laue Remembers

Beth Laue and Ruth 2006

My husband was the pastor of Calvary Bible Church in Burbank, California, for twenty-three years, beginning in 1975. Ruth had come to California with Chosen People Ministries in 1973. She began visiting our church and became a member. Once we got to know Ruth, we saw that she was a very capable teacher. We asked if she would teach our women's class. We wanted her to teach an eight-week series of lessons in the fall or spring during the week. She agreed to teach, and this became Ruth's main ministry at Calvary. Ruth was and is a fabulous teacher, although she would never say so since she is so humble. The thing I remember most is that Ruth always assigned memory verses, which was always a challenge for me. However, I still remember many of these verses some thirty years later. One of the women told me that she will never forget one thing that Ruth had said to the class. Ruth had told the class, "If it doesn't count for eternity, then it just doesn't matter."

Barbara Allard—Memories

I met "Ruth with the Truth" Wardell in January of 1981. She came to teach our Thursday morning Bible Study at Calvary Bible Church. Beth Laue had recommended that we ask her to do a series. She said that Ruth was a missionary, a woman who loved the Word of God and a great communicator. I don't remember if she mentioned that she was a missionary to the Jews at that time, but it only took a short time at our first session for Ruth to let her heart for the Chosen People become evident.

Barbara Allard

I loved the way that Ruth would always have a memory verse for us to learn during the week. Each week, she would review the previous week's memory verse. She would print them out on eight-by-ten-inch sheets of paper, and as the class would recite the verse, in Ruth Wardell style, she would grandly fling the paper over her shoulder. Even though she knew very few of the ladies who attended the Bible Study, they were sure to get a big hug from Ruth as a greeting. One day, Ruth either forgot or misquoted something, and when she realized what she had done, she laughed heartily and announced that her *faux pas* was the result of her being a member of the "HAG Society." Then she went on to share that eventually every woman would become a member of this group. She then informed us that HAG meant, Hardening of the Arteries Girls.

The next class that I took with Ruth was called "Competent to Counsel." Little did I know then that Ruth had almost no idea of what to teach. When she gave an assignment, she would do so with a great air of authority, and we would all follow her instructions. We thought that if "Ruth with the Truth" said something, then it must be so. One of the things that I appreciate about Ruth is the manner she displays when leading or teaching a group of people. I think she has more chutzpa (Yiddish for extreme boldness) than anyone I have ever known.

This boldness was even more evident to me in 1984 when Ruth was diagnosed with cancer. She began a journey of facing her affliction head on. She began to research everything that she could find about the treatment of this disease. She decisively chose the method of treatment and boldly endured the process of bringing the cancer into remission. Although she was often sick, tired, and weak, I witnessed this amazing lady fulfill each and every commitment she had, one day at a time. When asked how things were going, her usual response was, "The Lord and I are doing just fine."

"Ruth with the Truth" had also met my family, which includes a special-needs daughter, Gerri. Ruth opened her heart to Gerri. She somehow knew just how to reach my daughter, letting her be just who she was and always seeking to encourage her. Ruth introduced Gerri to her Bible Study group of Jewish ladies out in the Valley, and Gerri quickly grew to love those women. To Gerri, Ruth is known as "Grandma," and no better grandma could anyone want for this special woman.

Ruth continued to teach our Thursday morning Bible studies for many years, and it was through these studies that I learned to love the Old Testament. One year, Ruth was teaching some lessons in Proverbs, and about mid-way through the study, she wanted to emphasize the importance of Wisdom, Understanding, and Knowledge. True to form, she presented these words in the form of an acronym, WUK, and loudly proclaimed, "Now ladies, I want all of you to have a WUKy week." This is one I have often asked her about, "Are you having a WUKy week?" Her response is, "How about you?

Retirement?

Jews for Jesus (1988 – 1991)

In 1987, Chosen People Ministries decided to put the old-time missionaries out to pasture. While they appreciated what we had accomplished over the previous decades, they believed that the "old-timers" would not know how to relate to the new, young couples that were coming into the mission. This was somewhat disturbing to me and my experienced colleagues, since experienced workers were and still are sorely needed in missions work, especially Jewish missions work. I prayed for guidance, and the Lord promised that He would take care of me. This encouragement gave me the peace that I needed to leave Chosen People Ministries after forty-one years of service. I felt that this was God's way of telling me to move on.

Ruth in a Skit

Jews for Jesus was founded in 1973 by Moishe Rosen, who had once worked for ABMJ. Jews for Jesus is best known for its bold street evangelism of the Jewish people. The missionary workers for Jews for Jesus were studying for eight weeks during the summer at Fuller Seminary in California in order to receive a Master's degree in Jewish Studies. The children of those workers needed to be cared for while their parents were attending classes. The current President of Chosen People Ministries, Mitch Glaser, was working for Jews for Jesus at that time. Mitch and I were friends. I had known him when he was in his early twenties in New Jersey. At that time, he was attending Northeastern Bible College. He was one of the leaders of Jews for Jesus, and he came to me and said, "You know that we need somebody to be the principal of this school that we set up for the children of our missionaries. Would you consider it?" I immediately recognized that God was opening a door for me. At that time, I was still working as a volunteer with the older people at Chosen People Ministries, but I knew that at the "young" age of sixty-four, God still had work for me to accomplish. My age was not a problem for me. I still had good strength and stamina. I was able to get well-qualified teachers, and Mitch Glaser told me to develop a plan for this school.

Lyn Bond (Rosen), Daughter of Moishe Rosen (Founder of Jews for Jesus) Recalls

At the end of the 1980s, my husband and I were transferred to Los Angeles with Jews for Jesus, and Ruth was working there with Chosen People Ministries. We were embarking on a Master's degree program with the School of World Missions. Jewish studies were the focus, and we were working toward a degree in theology. It was a pilot program, and Jews for Jesus sent many missionary couples there to study. At that time, Ruth was retired from Chosen People Ministries. My dad, Moishe Rosen, who had worked with Ruth for years with CPM and knew her work, said to me, "You need to go and talk to Ruth about helping you put together a program for our children." Ultimately, the program, called "Messiah's Moshav," came to fruition, and Ruth became the principal. (*Moshav* means "a place of habitation; a cooperative settlement.")

This school needed to develop plans for a school day that started at 8 a.m. and ended at 5 p.m. Lessons were written to teach the children Hebrew, music, art, Jewish history, and Bible study. This would educate the children while at the same time keeping their interest. This was a wonderful situation since Ruth had all of this experience working with children. She had a really great attitude about kids. She just loved them in the way that Yeshua, Jesus, would love them. She really lived by the ideas that Jesus taught when He said, "Let the little children come to Me." She has always had her arms open for everybody. Our children still have the Messiah's Moshav scrapbook that they made during those summers with Ruth.

Messiah's Moshav

I prepared for the Messiah's Moshav program in 1987, and I ran the school for Jews for Jesus for four years from 1988 to 1991. The children attended from 8 a.m. until 5 p.m. every weekday. Our class hours were from 8 a.m. until noon, when we would have lunch, followed by play time. The first year went extremely well, and the number of children increased in the second year. In the final year of 1991, there were eighty children attending the summer school.

The school was located in Pasadena the first two years, and then was moved to Reseda, near North Hollywood, which is in the valley. I enjoyed every minute of the four years that I headed this school. I love to plan and organize things, and this position gave me this opportunity to do so. We taught the Bible, Hebrew, Jewish music, arts, play-drama, Jewish history, Jewish customs, and Messianic prophecy. The children's favorite activity was recess when we had snacks and play time. The way the school was organized was that the teachers were in one place, and the children moved from one teacher to the next throughout the day. The teachers would teach the same topic for all four teaching periods. The grade level of the lesson would change depending on the age group at any specific time. This was more efficient for the teachers, since they did not have to prepare for four different lessons each day. They focused on only one subject and taught it four times. The teachers were happy, and they were able to adapt to whatever had to be done. All I had to do was provide the textbooks and materials.

Many of the children that I taught in this school grew up to become workers for Jews for Jesus. In 2005, David Brickner, who now heads Jews for Jesus, met up with me. He told me about the children that I had taught during those four summers. At a meeting, David asked them, "What was the biggest thing that helped you throughout your lives growing up with Jews for Jesus?" They unanimously answered, "The Messiah's Moshav program." It pleased me to know that God had used the school to have some influence in their lives.

Mitch Glaser

Mitch Glaser is currently the President of Chosen People Ministries. I knew Mitch before he became part of Jews for Jesus back in 1971, when he was still going to Bible school in New Jersey. After Bible school, Mitch began working for Jews for Jesus, and he was my boss during the four years in California that I worked in the Messiah's Moshav school for the missionaries' children. I really enjoyed working with him, and it was at that time that I really got to know him well. I was also blessed to get to know his wife and children. It was a very good thing in my life to be with all of those people in Jews for Jesus.

When Mitch left Jews for Jesus, he came to visit with me in Texas, and we have been close ever since. I think that he has done a wonderful job bringing Chosen People Ministries back up after some down years.

Mitch Glaser—Memories

Dr. Mitch Glaser

I knew Ruth as a person who always rose above it all. She never had a bad word about anybody. She was always positive and encouraging. We had a nice relationship that was not particularly close, but it was warm. During those years, Ruth was an example of someone who was faithful and someone I admired greatly.

I created a Master of Arts program in Intercultural Studies for the major in Jewish Evangelism at Fuller Seminary. It was a summer program, and my goal was to have all of the Jews for Jesus (JFJ) staff go through this program because many of our workers had not been formally trained. We would bring ten or fifteen JFJ workers and their families to Pasadena every summer. Of course, this meant that there would be a lot of kids who would have to be cared for while their parents were attending class or studying.

Ruth had just retired from Chosen People Ministries, but by no means was she ready to stop working. This was a great coincidence for me. I needed to develop a children's program, and a person with decades of experience was now available. I asked Ruth if she would help develop and head the summer program that we called "Messiah's Moshav." This brought Ruth and I into a wonderful, close working relationship that has lasted until today. We worked together to design the program, hire the teachers, and rent the place for the classes. It was incredibly involved and took lots of time and effort. We had as many as forty to fifty children each summer. One year, it was held in Pasadena. Another year, it was in the San Fernando Valley. We had a wonderful program where we taught the children Hebrew, Bible, and other subjects. Ruth's abilities as an administrator, a lover of children, a teacher, and a mentor to staff was very impressive. The long-lasting impact that she had on these children was phenomenal. I can cite many of these children who are still walking with the Lord today as young adults, as well as others who have followed their parents into the ministry, all as a result of their interaction with Ruth.

Ruth and I kept up our relationship. When I left Jews for Jesus, I went to work with Ariel Ministries and Dr. Arnold Fruchtenbaum for fifteen months. Ruth helped me profoundly when I had to once again go out and raise my missionary support. I can recall at least two times that I went and stayed at Ruth's home in Texas. Ruth introduced me to churches and people and encouraged me incredibly when I began with Ariel. This was a time that I had become discouraged with ministry work and could have turned my back and walked away from it. Ruth was one of maybe five people who really saw me through the tough times and allowed me to get my joy back for missions work.

I left Ariel Ministries to become President of Chosen People Ministries. A few years after this, I was looking for someone who had a heart for the Chosen People retirees. I asked Ruth if she would take on the responsibility of having a phone ministry to the retirees and their families. Ruth agreed, and she calls the retirees every month. She then sends a report which is printed in the Chosen People Ministries internal staff letter *The Yenta*. *Yenta* is Yiddish for "someone who likes to gossip." This gives the retirees the sense that they are still involved with the mission. Essentially, Ruth is the CPM pastor to the retirees. If people are sick, she sends out prayer requests and calls them to pray with them and encourage them. Ruth has been invaluable in that way.

CHAPTER 16
Texas
(1993 – Present)

Leaving California—My New Home in Texas

After twenty years in California, I started to get restless to go back to the East again. I had finished my work with CPM and also the school with Jews for Jesus. I now wanted to be able to visit with my brother, my friends in Canada where I grew up, and my friends in New York. I was about seventy years old.

But I wanted to live where it was warm, since I had lived in California for twenty years. I was not excited about living where it was really cold and snowy in the winter. I especially needed a place where I could do ministry for the Lord. This was my first goal for moving. Some of the people I had known for many years in Chosen People Ministries and Jews for Jesus had moved to Texas, so I felt that there would be a place for me to teach if I went there. I would also have a lot of fellowship and not feel lonely in a new place. I began to pray and had my friends pray that the Lord would guide me to the place He would have for me.

I came to Plano, Texas, a town just north of Dallas, to look for a house to buy. My friends had contacted a realtor to help me, and we started out to look for a new home. I thought I would like to live in a condominium, but most of them were two stories high, and I felt that the stairs might prove difficult in years to come. In Texas, they have houses on what they call "zero lots." This makes it easy to take care of them since there is very little yard. As we were driving along, we saw one of these houses for sale. It was a lovely new house. The neighbors were out planting flowers, and I got to share some conversation with them. The house had been for sale for about six months, and they had reduced it $4,000 to entice someone to buy it.

I got my friend, who knew a great deal about buying houses, to come and look the house over. He felt it would be a good place. I had only four days in which to buy a house, so on the second day we signed the papers to buy this home. In the meantime, my house in California was on the market. I prayed that it would sell quickly. A young couple came and loved what they saw and decided to buy it. The money for the California house was in the bank just a short time before we needed it. The Lord, in His time, orchestrated the buying of the house here in Texas. Praise the Lord many times over.

My Texas Neighbors

The Ludgars

Ruth and the Ludgar Family

I am so thankful for the very precious neighbors that the Lord has given to me. Neighbors can mean a lot when you live alone. The Ludgars are my next-door neighbors. Janet is a nurse, and Edgar is a physical therapist. Their children, Brenna and Grant, are my "foster" grandchildren, and they call me "Grandma Moses." Janet is very kind, and she often brings something for me to eat for dinner. This is especially a blessing to me, since I am not fond of cooking.

Janet Ludgar's Comments

Ruth is the godliest woman that I have ever known. She has remarkable insight and wisdom. She is witty, but she knows when to be serious. She is our neighbor and friend. She is "Ruth with the Truth" and our very own "Grandma Moses." I remember the first time I met Ruth. She was looking for a house to buy, and she stopped with her realtor and asked me about the neighborhood. Shortly after that, she became our wonderful neighbor. That was in 1993, two years before our first child was born. Before we had children, Edgar and I were on vacation, and we sent Ruth a postcard with the name "Grandma Moses" on it to her address. Much to our delight, she told us that she actually liked being called "Grandma Moses."

When our daughter and son were little babies, Ruth would come over at least once a week to see them. As they grew older and they would see her in the yard, they would start squealing in delight for "Grandma Moses." She has been a surrogate grandmother to them. She has attended Grandparents Day with them at their school. They love her like a grandmother. It has been especially sweet to watch the relationship that has developed between Ruth and our daughter. Ruth is a friend and, I believe, a spiritual mentor to her.

We love Ruth! She has richly blessed us by her presence for the last seventeen years, right next to us in our neighborhood. I know God put her there. She prays daily for us, and I know we will see the fruit of that prayer in our children's lives for many years to come.

Bella Borgen

Bella Borgen met Edgar Ludgar when he was on a trip to Israel. Bella has an Orthodox Jewish background. As a young child, she lived in the U.S. for almost twenty years before moving to Israel for the last ten years. Bella ceased following the Orthodox faith about five years ago. When she came to my home the first time, she was not at all favorable to hearing about Jesus. She came to me in June of 2009. Happily, I found out that she accepted the Lord in August. She is giving a very strong testimony for Jesus, her Messiah, and loves to go to church to hear the Word and to sing about Jesus.

Bella Borgen Writes

My first encounter with Ruth was last June when I came to the U.S. from Israel for a short visit. Edgar Ludgar, a neighbor of Ruth's, introduced me to her. I needed a place to stay for that week, and Ruth welcomed me with open arms. I felt blessed, for she is a person who has worked and still is working with Jewish people for the past sixty years. As for me, being a Jew myself, we made an instant connection.

Ruth and Bella, 2009

During that visit with Ruth, I learned and heard a lot about Jesus. My stubbornness would not allow me to open up to the idea that Jesus is my Messiah, but Ruth didn't give up! She tried—oh, she did try! When it was time for me to return to Israel, I was confused, and it was difficult for me to sort out everything that I had learned about Yeshua, Jesus. Before I left, I got a New Testament, which I read on the long plane trip back to Israel. Surprisingly, I accepted Jesus into my heart in August. It is very simple to accept Jesus as your Savior, yet it is difficult to let go of the past. It is written in the New Testament, in Luke 11:9, "And I tell you, ask and it will be given to you, seek and you will find, and knock and it will be opened to you." I looked at the door in my apartment and said, "Jesus, if You say You enter, just please enter into my heart." At that moment, I knew that my sins were forgiven and all my stress that I had felt had been released. This happened sooner than I thought it would.

Once I was back in Israel, I found that I was feeling emptier each passing day. I needed guidance, so I decided to return to Ruth in Texas. I left everything behind, and Ruth was kind enough to open her door for me again. Ruth gave me the guidance that I so desperately needed and wanted. I also had difficulty with the idea of baptism being performed in public. Ruth, in her kindness and care, took the time to explain to me the reason why we get baptized and the importance of it. I did surrender in the end.

The room that I sleep in at Ruth's home is called "The Chapel." Ruth teaches Sunday classes for children in this room. For me, this house is not only a place to live in, it is also a chapel that I call home!

The Chinese Church

In Dallas, from 2005 to 2009, I taught a class of children at a Chinese Church founded by Dr. Paul Lee Tan, a noted author and Bible scholar. He had written a great book on prophecy and was a good friend of my brother Don. He had stayed in one of my brother's apartments when he was going to seminary in Indiana. When my brother died, Dr. Tan called me and wanted to know if he could come over and pray with me because he was sad, as my brother had been a great friend of his.

About four years ago, I went over to visit in his church, and they had a need for a teacher. It didn't take much coaxing, and I agreed to teach a class of preteens. I had a chapel time with music, then a Bible study. The Chinese children are very smart. They love to come to class. We made up a name for ourselves: Youth in Fellowship.

It is interesting to note that my parents had desired to go to China as missionaries, but due to circumstances, they never did. Here I was, decades later, working with Chinese people in the heart of Texas.

Dr. Paul Lee Tan Remembers

Ruth is in her eighth decade but has the energy of a much younger woman. We respect her for her maturity, experience, and loving ways with God's people. We all love her in the Chinese church. Our daughter Christine considers Ruth her mentor and spiritual advisor, and Christine feels free to share with her on many things.

**Dr. Paul Lee Tan and Ruth
2007**

Presently, even as my wife and I are in the Philippines, serving as missionaries, Ruth continues to faithfully and lovingly help out at the little Chinese church. We feel that God has brought Ruth into our lives for a purpose. That purpose is to encourage me and my family in Christian service and to continue helping in the Chinese work in Dallas as God enables.

"Ruth with the Truth" will always be a part of our family's spiritual heritage. We all thank God for raising up such an effective and humble servant of His in these Last Days.

Ministering to the Chinese People

Dr. Paul Tan's Daughter, Christine Tan, Writes

Christine Tan

Ms. Ruth Wardell is God's gift to Grace Chinese Church (Dallas) and to me personally. Our children's ministry had a need for a Sunday School teacher, and Ruth cheerfully accepted our invitation. Always the quintessential missionary, Ruth adapted quickly to our Chinese-speaking congregation and endeared herself to our entire group. Even at eighty-plus years of age, she could relate instantly to any age of children and youth. The young professionals and mature-age people also flocked to her.

We taught Ruth how to enjoy Chinese food (like dim sum and mooncake) and various facets of Chinese culture. And she, in turn, shared her great knowledge of the Bible, especially its Jewish aspects. In our years together, I have never heard discouraging or disparaging remarks from her lips. I personally consider Ms. Ruth Wardell a spiritual mentor, an excellent example of a true missionary, and one of my dearest friends.

Ruth Writes

It has been wonderful to get to know the Tan family. Paul Tan is one of the finest pastors I know, and other than my own mother, his wife Helen, is the best pastor's wife I have ever been acquainted with. I praise God for this experience.

Terry Kanter—Memories

Ruth Wardell has been mother, grandmother, mentor, and friend to me for over twenty years. I met Ruth when I was a very young believer, only about one year old in the Lord. God had led me to the Los Angeles offices of Chosen People Ministries, and Ruth made me feel that I was welcome and was a vital part of the staff and ministry there. I was immediately impressed by her joy in the Lord. It was amazing to me that at the time I met her, she was battling her first round of cancer. I would never have guessed that she was going through such a heavy trial. It was only because the office manger had told me of Ruth's struggle that I knew about it. She was so full of love and joy that it impressed me greatly. Ruth exemplified a life of sacrificial service for the cause of the Gospel.

Ruth has also been a great witness to my husband John's unsaved family, especially his mom. It is Ruth's encouragement, prayers, and testimony that have kept me going so many times when I might have given up. There are people whom Ruth has loved and ministered to for years who have been unkind or even cruel to her. Yet, she has never returned evil for evil. Instead, she has continued to love them and pray for them. That is how Jesus loves, not expecting anything in return, just loving people for the sake of the Messiah. What an example she is of the love of Jesus.

Terry Kanter

Ruth lives what she teaches, and what she teaches is the joy of a life lived in obedience to the will of God and to the truth of His Word. I count Ruth as one of the biggest blessings that God has given to me this side of heaven.

Zav and Margie Masoomian Remember

Marge and Zav Masoomian

We first met Ruth on Long Island at Levittown Baptist Church around 1960. Her mother was my Sunday School teacher. She quickly discovered that I did not have the Lord in my life. She asked me to her home for tea. It was through that experience that I gave my heart to Jesus and became a believer. I met Ruth through her mother. One Sunday morning, after church had started, I saw Ruth stalking down the aisle as if she were the only one in the church. She came and sat down next to her mother. Her mother instructed her to be quiet. I wanted to know who this person was that stalked down the aisle after church had started.

Ruth's mother once told me, "Always be hospitable when you have people over to your house." This is something that Ruth does often and quite well. She can have people over and have a colorful, delicious meal on the table at the drop of a hat. She can make a meal of all healthy foods. Her salads are scrumptious and satisfying.

If you have one good friend, you are rich. For me, that friend would be Ruth Wardell. She is a true friend. If I had to go to the hospital, when I opened my eyes, she was there. Ruth is just as active today as she ever was. I don't know how she does it, but God must give her the strength to keep going.

[Editor's note: Marge passed away on August 18, 2008.]

CHAPTER 17
Ruth's Musings/Reflections

Doing the Will of God

Every evening when I go to bed, I ask, "Lord, did I do Your will today?" Invariably He will tell me, "You didn't in this or that situation." Then I say to the Lord, "I'm sorry. I'll do better tomorrow." I find that if people do not do this, they can find themselves out of the will of God, and that is not a good place to be. It just doesn't pay, since when one is out of the will of God, things just don't seem to work out quite right. I find that when I keep close watch on doing God's will, it works for me every time. I find myself asking Him this question during the day, not just at bedtime. Thank God for His Spirit that tells us when we have missed it.

Reflections on Life

It was in the fall of 1983. Things were going well, and people were coming to know the Lord and being blessed, when out of nowhere, I had a lump in my breast. I went to the doctor and because of the size and the texture of the lump, he immediately sent me for x-rays. The results were positive for cancer, and we needed to do something quickly.

On entering the Presbyterian Hospital for the x-ray, I saw a verse printed from the Bible in the lobby. It said: "As for God, His way is perfect." 2 Samuel 22:31. It came with strong feelings that I was in the way of perfection, and nothing can happen to me that God does not already know about, and in His mercy He will take care of all things. Looking back, it was a wonderful experience of knowing *peace* in the midst of what could have been a big storm. It was wonderful that with this perspective I was able to comfort my friends who feared that I would not come through this time of trouble.

After the operation, the doctor told me that the cancer had not gone into the lymph nodes, and consequently, the chances of a full recovery were good. My friends were really joyful about that. I had the prescribed six weeks of radiation therapy. Back in 1983, they gave a lot more radiation than they do today, just in case the surgery might have missed something. How I thank the Lord for the caring friends who made those days so much easier to bear.

A short while after the operation, I developed a bad case of shingles. Shingles is a condition where the nerves are attacked by a virus. I read in my devotional book that instead of looking at what you have, and perhaps feeling sorry for yourself, you should look at what God is doing in your life to comfort you through the trial that you are having. I took a notebook and started writing down all of the lovely things that the Lord did to help me through this trial. It was such an encouragement to me that my attitude changed, and I was able to bless others with an attitude of thanksgiving to the Lord for *all* that He was doing in sending people to comfort and bless me through this time of illness. This idea of always looking at how God comforts us instead of looking at our illnesses has stayed with me, and it has greatly helped me every time I have had a need.

In 2003, in Texas, I was diagnosed with cancer for a second time. This time it was caught very early, and after a couple of operations and five-and-a-half weeks of radiation, all was well. A lady named Linda took me home after the first operation and gave me a great deal of comfort. Many people came to help. Some drove me to receive radiation treatments. Others brought food. I was greatly blessed and much encouraged for all the care the Lord provided. I thank the Lord that the radiation was not as intense as it had been the first time. God, in His Mercy, helped me learn to really trust Him.

God Prepares Us for Ministry

Gladys Carey

Many things that happen to us have a definite value to help us in future situations. When I was seventeen, my parents took care of an elderly woman named Mrs. Marwood, who was the grandmother of my second cousin Gladys Carey.

Gladys Writes

Ruth's parents, Glen and Maude Wardell, very kindly took into their home my grandmother, Lizzie Marwood. This was because my parents, Harold and Amy Dancy, had gone back to Nigeria as missionaries. We knew there was something wrong with Grandma, but unlike now, my parents weren't encouraged to stay at home to look after their parents.

Mrs. Lizzie Marwood

Lizzie Marwood was an older woman with what we now diagnose as Alzheimer's disease. She would forget everything and lose all her things. If she could not find things, she would accuse us of taking them. My mother seemed to have a hard time adjusting to her. I spent quite a bit of time with her and found that the best way to help her was just to agree with her. After a few months, Mrs. Marwood would go out and become lost, and the policemen would bring her home. Soon after this, my father found a nice place for her to stay where they could properly take care of her.

When I went to New York in 1946, Miss Sussdorf, whom we talked about before, was beginning to display some symptoms of Alzheimer's. The workers would try to correct her errors, and it led to a lot of confusion on Miss Sussdorf's part. We would take her every week to the doctor. I remembered my time with Mrs. Marwood, and I knew that it was best to just agree with everything Miss Sussdorf said. We became good friends and had some happy times together. However, looking back, if I did not have the time with Mrs. Marwood, I would not have been able to help Miss Sussdorf. It was a good lesson in life to see how God prepares us in one thing so that we might serve Him with the lessons we have learned in another place. Wow! God in His mercy really shows us the way to go each day in our lives.

Messianic Congregations

I believe that Messianic Congregations have their place. They all need a little something such as discipleship as an ongoing course along with other things. I believe that what congregations forget to do sometimes is to put Jesus at the center of everything. They must continually ask themselves, "Who are we following?" and "Are we following traditions? We can do that, but who's first? Where do we settle on who's first and what we are doing?" We should be following and loving Jesus and serving Jesus. That's what we did in New York and in the North Hollywood Mission in California.

At first, people told me that the Jewish people would not come if we placed Jesus first. I disagreed and said, "Oh yes, they will." I was right. One must consider the question, "Where does the power come from?" The answer is the power comes from the Spirit of God that lives in us and from the Word of God and from Jesus Himself. That's it. Unfortunately, I do not see this in congregations as often as I would like to see it.

The Place in Jewish Ministries for Gentile Believers

In Jewish evangelism, the majority of Jewish people who came to faith started out with a witness from a Gentile believer. We are told in the Scripture to "provoke them to jealousy." (Romans 11:11 says, "I say then, Did they stumble that they might fall? God forbid: but by their fall salvation is come unto the Gentiles, to provoke them to jealousy.") The way we provoke Jewish people to jealousy is by demonstrating our faith and showing our enthusiasm and love for the Jewish Messiah. This is something that every one of us can do. Over and over, in witnessing to Jewish people, I have seen this happen. Once a Jewish person was "provoked to jealousy," I would bring in a Jewish believer, like Dr. Vera Schlamm to help the Jewish person understand that one could still be Jewish *and* believe in Jesus.

Dr. Vera Schlamm Comments

One of the things that I have always shared with people in the churches is that they are mistaken if they believe that Jewish believers are the ones who should witness to Jewish unbelievers. Gentile believers are the ones who have the better chance of sharing the Gospel with their Jewish friends, neighbors, and co-workers. Jewish people will not listen to Jewish believers like me because they see us as traitors. Gentile believers can help to lead them to the Lord, and then when they come to faith, the Jewish believer can be instrumental in discipling them. I have found that sometimes I can come in when they are on the brink of accepting Jesus and encourage them that they are not doing anything wrong and that it is okay to be Jewish and a believer in Jesus.

Change in Methodology

Today, many Messianic Congregations and some Jewish missions are made up of mostly Gentile believers. As a result, the Jewishness of the Gospel has been minimized or totally lost. Back in the 1940s and 1950s, the mission was attended by an exclusively Jewish population which made up ninety-five percent of those attending the different functions sponsored by the mission. Having mostly Jewish believers in the mission made my work easier than it might be today. When teaching the Bible to Jewish people, I didn't have to explain the Jewish culture since they already knew it quite well. It wasn't that the Jewish missions didn't want Gentiles to attend and come to faith. On the contrary, all were welcome. However, it was and is the goal of the mission to reach out to the Jewish people and to share the Gospel so that they may come to faith.

Managing and Giving Finances

I had been working for ABMJ, and I remember that after giving ten dollars to the Lord, I had the "great sum" of ninety dollars to live on for the month. I quickly learned how to manage this meager paycheck. After paying for room and board, I may have had fifteen dollars left each week. This had to cover the fare for the subways that I traveled to and from work, my clothes, and anything else that I may have needed. I obviously did well at managing money as I soon had $250 in my bank account. When I was growing up, people didn't save any money. If someone had a surplus, they gave it away because we believed that the Lord wanted us to give it to help the needy. If you had some extra money, you blessed someone with it. I still wonder about our modern society. Everyone saves and saves for retirement, but they don't really practice giving sacrificially.

Years ago, people were more in tune with God. If God said to give money to someone, one acted obediently. Here I was with a savings of $250. While I was sitting alone one day, I prayed, "Lord, I have $250. I need to give it to somebody. Whoever you want me to give this to, I will give it." A short time later I was impressed to give this money to a lady named Beatrice who was a missionary to the Jewish people. Beatrice and I had gone to the London Bible Institute together and were in the same class. She was doing work in Phoenix, Arizona. I sent her a letter informing her that I was going to send the $250 to her. Unbeknownst to me, Beatrice had been praying for exactly this amount because she needed to buy a car. Beatrice suffered from severe bronchitis, and she could no longer walk very far. She prayed and God answered her prayer through me. Beatrice died a few years later, sometime in the 1950s. Her sister sent a check to me for more than $300 from the estate that Beatrice had somehow accumulated. This is how God has always worked in my life. The Bible says in Luke 6:38, "Give, and it will be given unto you." It happens each time.

Memorizing Scriptures

Early Childhood

Since early childhood, I have had the joy of memorizing Scriptures. My father was very good at setting up programs where we learned a lot of verses. It has been a blessing beyond measure to memorize God's Word, and it certainly helps to keep one on the path of righteousness. Since the Word of God really equals the will of God, when you memorize it and do it, you are doing the will of God. This made memory work very precious to me.

Messianic Prophecies

When I first became a missionary in New York, I was thrilled to see all of the Old Testament passages pointing to Jesus being the Jewish Messiah. I started with the birth of Jesus and memorized the verses that had to do with His life, death, resurrection, second coming, etc. It was a glorious experience, and it really strengthened my faith to see the fulfillment of so many wonderful prophecies. It was also a great help in witnessing to Jewish people.

A Chapter a Week

To effectively memorize Scripture and to enjoy the process, it is good to have a partner that you are accountable to for learning the verses. The first time I had the joy of doing this was with a lady named Peggy. We were challenged by Bill Gothard of the Institute of Basic Youth Conflicts to memorize a chapter a week, then pray the Scripture back to God, and to live each verse day by day. Peggy and I did this for almost two years from 1970 – 1972. We both grew in the Lord in a remarkable way. I can still remember many times when the Word of God convicted me of not really obeying the things that God wanted me to do. In Psalm 1:2, we are told to "meditate day and night in the Scriptures." This really happened to Peggy and me, especially if the chapters were quite long, like forty or more verses. Looking back, that was a great time in my life. It was a blessing beyond measure.

One Hundred Scriptures per Year

The latest joy of memorizing Scripture came with my friend Evelyn Bridges who lives in Indiana. In five years, we memorized over 500 verses.

After I retired to Texas, I used to visit my brother Don in Indiana during the summer months. While I was out walking one evening, I stopped by the house of Evelyn Bridges, who was one of Don's neighbors I had come to know.

Evelyn Writes

Ruth and Evelyn Bridges

One evening when Ruth was out walking, she came by my house to visit. We chatted for a while. She asked me if I knew of anyone who would like to study God's Word, commit Scripture verses to memory, and be accountable to her, and she would be accountable to them. I told Ruth that I would love to do that. I had been praying for a friend with whom I could share the Scriptures.

Evelyn wasn't quite sure that she could do that kind of memorization. Then I quoted Philippians 4:13, "I can do all things through Christ who strengthens me." I asked her, "Do you think Jesus wants you to study and memorize His Word?" Evelyn said, "Oh, yes. He wants us to hide His Word in our heart that we might not sin against Him." (Psalm 119:11). We both said that we would pray. When I returned to her house, I had printed out verses on big sheets of paper in big letters. When the thought of the verse would change, I changed the color of the ink. Evelyn found this a very enticing, non-threatening method of learning. It was just something that she wanted to do.

We memorized more than 500 verses together over a period of five years. Each week, we would speak by telephone and recite the verses together. We were both blessed beyond measure to share God's Word together.

Donna Klein Writes

Working with Miss Ruth at the close of her ministry is quite an experience. I watch her consistently challenge young and old "students" alike to memorize Scriptures. There's no question that she believes it is vital to a well-balanced spiritual life, and you can certainly see the living proof of it in hers.

I first met Ruth at a women's Bible study held by our congregation. I didn't know much about her except that she was a retired Chosen People's missionary. I don't remember much about the study but was inspired to start memorizing Bible verses. Since I'd been unsuccessful at earlier attempts, I asked her for some advice. Much to my surprise, she said she'd help me. So, with a goal of 100 verses in a year, we got started. At first, Miss Ruth gave me verses to learn, but as time progressed, I started choosing them on my own. We'd meet every week to go over what I'd learned. First, I'd recite some of the older ones, then I'd say some of the newer ones. I quickly learned that no excuses were allowed. She always encouraged me to do better. She'd remind me that nothing was more important.

Her approach was a little on the inductive side. If the verse was about something wonderful, she'd say, "Isn't that exciting! Now let's say it like we're excited!" And, I'd repeat the verse extra enthusiastically. Her encouraging and fun style helped me reach my goal rather painlessly. And we celebrated the "big event" with a dinner out.

If you have never tried memorizing Scriptures, please do. Find someone to whom you can be accountable and be responsible to hide God's Word in your heart. You will be blessed beyond measure.

Forgiveness

Mrs. Dugan

The Dugan Family

When I was young in Oshawa, our family became very friendly with one of the families at the church, the Dugan family. Mrs. Dugan had accepted the Lord under my father's preaching, and she was a great student of the Word and really appreciated my father's teaching and discipling over the years. She also loved and highly respected my mother, who helped her through many problems. Mr. Dugan also became a believer, and we had many wonderful times sharing together.

One time, Mr. Dugan became very ill, and he was having a lot of medical problems. The problems seemed to draw the family closer to Jesus. I was just a girl of about fourteen. I had a real desire to be close to Jesus, and I remember praying that if problems brought you closer to Jesus that I would like to have some. The Lord really answered that prayer some years later, for as a missionary to the Jewish people, there were many problems that came my way.

Our families stayed close over the years, sharing in each other's joys and sorrows.

Then my father passed away, and soon after, Mr. Dugan died. My mother came to live with me in New York. One weekend, Mrs. Dugan came to visit with us and brought a couple of friends with her. We had a wonderful time. I was really excited that she came, and we had some great times of fellowship, laughing, and remembering.

A short time after she returned to her home, she wrote a letter to me. During the weekend that she visited with us, I must have acted in a way that did not seem to be the way that a "missionary" should act, in her opinion. She wrote that she felt that my entire ministry was "wood, hay, and stubble," and that I needed "to shape up, confess my sins, and be different." I was rather taken aback at what she had said. I guess I had really cut up over the weekend to have received such a critical letter. I wrote to her and expressed to her that I was sorry that she felt that way. I shared a couple of blessings with her and then prayed that somehow the Lord would straighten out the problem.

Looking back at my life, I knew that she was wrong. The Lord was blessing me greatly in the work of the ministry. For example, on the Sunday night before she visited, I had taken a group of the young people to speak in a church. As usual, they gave their testimonies, and the people in the church were blessed abundantly and related so beautifully with the group.

In the years to come, I saw this woman on a couple of occasions when my mother and I went to speak in some churches in Canada. She was courteous to me but not friendly. Time passed, and my mother went to heaven. Three years later, in 1973, I went to California.

One Christmas, when I was in California, I wrote a letter to all of my friends. I wrote the beginning of a paragraph that read, "I remember . . . ." I then wrote about a pleasant memory from my life. After that paragraph of memories, I wrote, "What do you remember?" I left a space for them to write something they remembered. I wrote one of these to this dear woman in Canada who had been a good friend at one time. I really didn't know if she would respond, but surprisingly, she answered. She wrote, "I remember writing a letter to you many years ago, and I would like to ask your forgiveness for the things I said. I know, having watched you over the years, that the things I wrote in that letter were not true, and I ask you to forgive me." I felt as if something had swept over my soul. The hurt and sorrow caused by the letter she had written were now gone. One year later, she came to visit with me. It was a wonderful week, and she said that it was the best vacation of her life. I also had the opportunity to visit with her in Canada.

It took some time for this particular situation to clear up, but how I thank the Lord that He brought a solution to the problem and that the Holy Spirit showed her what she needed to do. This was a wonderful lesson to me of how the Lord can, in His way and time, solve our problems. Sometimes, just waiting and loving the person who hurts us brings wonderful results. Praise the Lord!

Helping People in Need

Besides evangelism, ministry also involves helping those who find themselves in the midst of many problems. One such lady was Toni. She had many needs, and God in His mercy brought her to Beth Sar Shalom in North Hollywood, where there was love and much fellowship that would help her find some direction for her life. She relates the following story.

Toni Remembers

My remembrances of Ruth Wardell go back to Los Angeles, when she was a missionary for Chosen People Ministries. I had moved from Chicago to L.A. in 1979. My marriage was on the rocks, and I didn't know what to do and had no friends. It was a very tough time. I looked in the phone book for Jewish ministries because I am a Jewish believer and found Chosen People. I phoned them and learned that there was a ladies' Bible class. That turned out to be Ruth's class. There were about thirty or more people there, and I began to attend each week.

Toni

Ruth was the most enthusiastic Bible teacher I've ever met. I love the Bible, and she loved the Bible more than I do. As I got to know Ruth, she began to counsel me. Her whole objective was to redirect my focus to the Lord instead of my problem marriage. Ruth then began to have me design her lesson plans for her—another attempt to divert my attention back to the Lord. She became a wonderful friend and perfect counselor and confidant. She had a terrific ministry going, and she involved me as much as she could with helping. I will always be thankful for her influence and especially for her uncanny ability to refocus whoever she talked with and remind them to turn to the Lord for all their needs.

It has been a very rewarding experience over the years to see so many people, like Toni, find answers to their problems as they sought the Lord and His wisdom to help them.

God Supplies Our Needs

It is always wonderful to see how God supplies our needs. During my first bout with cancer, I was quite ill. The Lord brought a dear friend to live with me. She was a great help in a multitude of ways. Her name was Raylene. She writes about the time we shared my home together.

Raylene

I moved from Portland, Oregon, to Sun Valley, California (near Burbank). I got a job interview with Chosen People Ministries. Dr. Goldberg was in charge of the center at the time, and he interviewed and hired me. I needed a place to live that was close to the Chosen People Ministries office in the San Fernando Valley. Ruth Wardell took me into her home. Ruth was like my mom-away-from-home and also a lot of fun as a dear friend. She had a lovely house in Reseda with a separate bedroom and bathroom off the kitchen, where I stayed.

Raylene

Living with Ruth was like living with a celebrity evangelist, a female version of Billy Graham. Having grown up in Canada as the child of a Baptist pastor, Ruth can talk, teach, and preach as well as anyone. From years of speaking in all kinds and sizes of churches in many countries, she has been blessed with a booming voice that can carry to the last pew of any church. People called on her at all times, day or night, for counseling. She knew all the people involved in early Jewish evangelism in the United States. Working for Chosen People Ministries in California was like the United Nations and more - people from Russia, Israel (a doctor who survived the Six-Day War), Holocaust survivors like Dr. Vera Schlamm, celebrities like Donna Jean Wood from Beverly Hills—they came to her Bible studies at the Center or visited her home. I also got to meet Ruth's friends who were Jewish believers, like Emily and others. What a privilege to meet these Jewish believers and experience their enthusiasm and love for Jesus. They really want to share the Good News.

Ruth had a Jacuzzi in the backyard. After a day of work and the aerobic class, we could sit in the Jacuzzi and talk about the day or whatever needed to be discussed and relax. It was truly wonderful to sit outside in the warm California night with the stars overhead. People in ministry need to keep fit to run the race. It seemed that no matter how ill Ruth might be at times, if she had a speaking engagement or commitment, she would pray and gather herself together somehow to meet her obligations and not disappoint the people who were counting on her.

The New York World's Fair

In 1964 – 1965, there was a World's Fair held at Flushing Meadow Park in Queens, New York. Chosen People Ministries had set up a booth there. World's Fairs are usually very well attended, and New York was, and still is, the city with the second largest population of Jewish people in the world. CPM took this booth to hand out literature and to witness to those who visited our booth.

Just behind Chosen People's Ministries' booth was a booth with Hasidic (ultra-Orthodox) Jews. They would come by, pick up one of our tracts, rip it to shreds, and throw it at us. They were not too happy with us, to say the least. This went on for quite some time until September/October arrived. It is at this time that we came into the Jewish High Holy days of Rosh Hashanah (the Jewish New Year) and Yom Kippur (the Day of Atonement.) The ten days between these two holidays is known to Jews as the "Ten Days of Awe." The Jewish people believe that, at this time of the year, God is determining the names of the people that will be written in the Book of Life for the upcoming year. No Jew wants to be left out of the Book of Life, so it is during these ten days that Jews are on their best behavior. Suddenly, these Jewish people, who had been very arrogant toward us, were extremely polite. They would greet us with a cheery, warm "Good morning!" and ask us how we were doing. For ten whole days, we had a very peaceful situation. As soon as Yom Kippur had passed, they were back to tearing up our literature and throwing it at us again.

We were there as a witness to the Jewish people. We distributed many, many tracts and books. We also had the opportunity to speak with many people that we otherwise might not have reached. It is a good thing that we had many workers at the fair. We needed them. There were many good and encouraging conversations, and some came to faith in their Messiah. Dorothy Franco was one who came to faith.

Dorothy Franco

This is the testimony of Dorothy Franco from *Ha-Adouth* (The Witness), January-March of 1967:

> I am a conservative, Sephardic Jew, whose parents come from Turkey. [*Editor's note*: Sephardic Jews are descended from the Jews of Spain, Portugal, and the Middle East]. I was always taught never to love the name of Jesus; as a matter of fact, my father told me it was a sin to say His name. He tried to encourage me not to read the Old Testament, but I would occasionally read it anyway, to question my father about it, who seemed to have an answer for everything I asked.

> I received a course in the mail which started with the Torah. This seemed very Jewish to me, so I decided to continue with it. On receiving the lessons, I was quite surprised by the titles; "Who Is the Jewish Messiah?" and "Daniel's 490-Year Prophecy." Now I thought I could tell my Christian friends something. I had read these words on Yom Kippur night and after finishing them, I was quite shaken. I had not even quite finished reading them yet when I realized the calculations in Daniel's 490 year prophecy coincided with the time Jesus was born and of His ministry. Overtaken by this, I decided to continue because I became very curious. Eventually I began to believe that Jesus was the Son of God, separate from God, and that He was the Messiah, but I could not understand how He could be God. I began to see many Old Testament prophecies concerning Jesus.

> Through prayer, I found my answer at the booth of the American Board of Missions to the Jews at the World's Fair where I met Mr. and Mrs. Kalmus.

> In a few short weeks, I was very easily able to understand how the Lord Jesus Christ was God.

Ruth's Comments

Dottie (as we called her) attended many of the functions of the Messianic Youth Fellowship. It was always a joy to see her.

Modern Education

I have spent most of six decades teaching children of all different ages. Each group of children is entirely different from the others. I believe that, today, too many children just sit in classrooms all over the country and don't learn much at all. Children don't know how to listen nowadays, and often, they don't even hear what you say to them. So much of what they have, such as computers, Game Boys, etc., are distractions. Children may go to their regular schools and may listen a bit to their lessons. When they are tested, they may receive a B or a C, and they are happy with that. They don't do much homework or make much of an effort. I believe that this is because we don't challenge the young people to use their God-given intelligence. Many times, I have just finished teaching a lesson, and the children do not seem to be able to answer even the most basic question about what they have just heard.

Bar Mitzvah Classes

I have been teaching a Bar Mitzvah class for children eleven to thirteen years old who attend the Messianic Jewish Congregation. It is a two-year course. In the Jewish culture, Bar Mitzvah literally means "son of the commandment." Technically, this refers to the age at which a child comes of age and is obligated to follow the commandments in the Torah (the first five Books of the Bible). This happens automatically when a boy reaches the age of thirteen and a girl becomes twelve years old.

Donna Klein with Bar Mitzvah Class, 2009

A child's training for their Bar/Bat Mitzvah includes teaching them Hebrew, their Torah portion, the Aaronic Benediction, Jewish History from Abraham to the present time, the covenants, Jewish traditions and holy days, and Messianic prophecies. I also feel that it is important for them as Jewish children to know why they believe in Jesus. By sharing the Messianic prophecies and the testimonies of Jewish people who have become believers in their Messiah, they will be prepared to share the reasons for their faith.

Anybody can have a party, but if they want to be Bar Mitzvah, they are going to have to push through and finish this course. They are going to learn their fifty, sixty, or seventy verses. They're going to have a good idea of what it means to believe in Jesus by the time they have finished. The congregation where I give lessons is a Messianic Jewish congregation. It is necessary to have Messianic teachings in the Bar Mitzvah class.

Karen Knoch Remembers

Ruth is so special to our family. Miss Ruth taught my two older children, Adam and Megan Anthony, through their Bar/Bat mitzvahs. She was always so dynamic and interesting. There was never a dull moment. At each Bar/Bat Mitzvah, as part of her speech to the birthday child, she would always make an acronym of the child's name and involve the whole congregation in repeating each one. Some were touching, and some made us laugh. There was always an air of excitement as to what Ruth was going to say about each letter of the child's name.

Carol Betten Recalls

Betten Children

God has blessed me with a wonderful husband, amazing children, and a loving extended family, but one of the greatest blessings in my life is knowing Ruth Wardell.

I first met Ruth when she came to Adat Shalom Messianic Congregation to work with the children. I found out she had been with Chosen People Ministries for a number of years. Soon, I discovered that she was a wonderful person who loved to have fun and was full of life. I knew that this was someone I needed to get to know better. Most people thought of her as this matriarchal figure, a godly woman who had led a faithful life through good and bad times. She was every bit of that, but I also came to know her very mischievous side, and I respected her even more! This "fun" side of Ruth is one of the many things that makes her so successful in her work with children—not to mention us fun-loving adults! She also has a special heart for working with active boys, probably because she grew up with a houseful!

In 1999, Ruth began to train my oldest son Daniel for his Bar Mitzvah. This was the first Bar Mitzvah to take place at our congregation in many years. It was a blessing for us and for Daniel to be taught by someone so knowledgeable and experienced in Jewish ministry, who could share personally about the many trials and God's continued faithfulness she had experienced over her many years. At Daniel's Bar Mitzvah, I said, "You know, Ruth, you did such a wonderful job with Daniel. You are just going to have to keep going until you have finished with Sarah." Sarah is the youngest of my four children and was four years old at the time. I truly wanted her to teach all my children, but I didn't really expect her to delay retirement so that all my children would get to work with her. But retirement is not in Ruth Wardell's vocabulary! Sarah's Bat Mitzvah was this year (2008), and though Ruth retired from her weekly Shabbat class teaching at Adat Shalom, she continues to give bi-weekly Bar/Bar Mitzvah classes in her home to the fortunate children who are now of age to sit under her teaching.

Daniel Betten - Bar Mitzvah

Miss Ruth, as I and so many other people have affectionately come to call her, has had a dramatic impact on my life. She was not only my Bar Mitzvah teacher for two years but also my Shabbat school teacher over four years. There is nothing like being taught by Miss Ruth. I have never been around anyone else with so much enthusiasm for learning about God's Word. When she speaks, her face lights up, and you cannot help but share in the energy as her enthusiasm spills over into your spirit. Whether it was a passage of Scripture or stories of how God has done amazing things in people's lives, her will to help people realize that God can do anything never wanes. Her hope is contagious, and that is the only way I can describe it. Even when she is speaking to the entire congregation, you can look around to see everyone captivated by her words, not necessarily because of her words, but because of the way she says them.

During my Bar Mitzvah training, we read many books that covered the breadth of Jewish history, and it still amazes me today how someone who is not Jewish can enjoy and help others to enjoy learning about their history so much. One of my favorite stories is about two Messianic believers centuries ago, who stood up to debate a hundred rabbis over the validity of their faith—and how God did not let them embarrass themselves.

Perhaps the biggest impact she has had on me, however, is in my daily walk with God. I have never met anyone who has so exhibited the character of Christ as she does, and it is an inspiration to me all the time. One of my memory verses from my training is Micah 6:8, "What does the Lord require of you, but to do justly, to love mercy, and to walk humbly with your God." Ruth definitely lives by that verse. Saying that I have been blessed by having Miss Ruth in my life would be odd to say, because there is nothing I could do to earn it; it is only by the grace of God that I have been privileged to know and to have been influenced by her. To me, she is not just my teacher but also my friend, and I consider her a part of my family.

Jackie Hager

Jackie Hager is one of the ladies at Adat Shalom Congregation. She helped in the teaching of the children's Bar/Bat Mitzvah classes. Jackie was well-loved by the children because of her infectious laughter and joyful spirit.

Jackie Writes

Jackie Hager

Upon being introduced to Ruth Wardell, I asked, "Are you *the* Ruth Wardell who led Arnold Fruchtenbaum to the Lord?"

"Yes," she said, "And I taught him everything he knows." She said it with a twinkle in her eye. We both know how much Arnold keeps in his head.

Meeting her was like being introduced to a pillar of the faith. Now in her early eighties, she is already a legend among Messianic Jews. Ruth and I attend the same congregation in Dallas, so I have watched her as she prepares eleven and twelve year olds for Bar and Bat Mitzvahs. Her "kids" always do well because she expects much from them. They are steeped in the Covenants, Israelology, Messianic prophecies, Jewish history and traditions, and memory work—often citing whole passages with ease. In an era of the "dumbing down" of America, Miss Ruth will settle for nothing less than excellence, and she gets it. Why? Because she knows exactly how to hold their attention. Her classes are grueling but fun. She moves from memory verses to discussions, from Bible drills to devotionals, from prayers to assignments. She writes plays that the children perform for the congregation. What is her secret? She *loves* every child placed in her care, and they love her back. She is fun-loving and energetic. She has high standards and an optimism for their success based on her complete faith in the God of Abraham to accomplish in each child a work of excellence.

Jean London

My son David prepared for his Bar Mitzvah with Ruth. For about two years, he went to her home each Tuesday afternoon. They studied, played games, and ate. Ruth put David's picture on her refrigerator and charted his height on her wall. This was a wonderful time for David.

David's Bar Mitzvah service was a wonderful experience for us. He had memorized his verses in English and Hebrew, recited them perfectly, and was relaxed and confident during

London Family

the entire service.

Five years later, my son Daniel started his Bar Mitzvah preparation. Ms. Donna assisted. Daniel also did well at his Bar Mitzvah.

My third son Ben started his Bar Mitzvah classes at Ruth's home a few weeks ago. He is enjoying his studies and learning his memory verses very well.

I was always impressed by Miss Ruth's interest in my sons and her willingness to teach them. She never seemed too tired or bored with the task. Even though my boys were not always interested in going to Ruth for classes, they always had a good time and came home energized.

Good Friends

Jeanette Lockerbie Johnston
(Mother of Jeanie Lockerbie Stephenson)

Jeanette Lockerbie

Life gives us many good friends. In the 1950s, I found a good friend in Jeanette Lockerbie Johnston, whom I affectionately always called, "Mrs. L." Jeanette was well known. She had authored many devotionals and biographies, and she spoke at many women's conferences around the country.

She was a caring friend to me. When I had cancer, she wrote me a note. She said, "I am sad." That little expression really struck me; someone was sad for *me*! On the last day of radiation, she came to my house to be with me and walk me through that day. I've never forgotten that. We had wonderful times together in our sharing. We shared our hurts and problems. We shared what the Lord can do through all of these things.

We trusted each other. We prayed together. We read the Bible together. We had that type of fellowship that comes rarely in a lifetime with a friend. I thank God that I was Mrs. Lockerbie Johnston's best friend and that she was my "Mrs. L."

Ben and Lisa Shapiro

I knew Ben as a young boy when he was enrolled in Jews for Jesus' summer program, Messiah's Moshav in Pasadena, California. Ben also attended the Messianic Congregation in Dallas that I attended.

Lisa Shapiro Writes

We were in church, and the sermon was on storing up your treasure in heaven while you are here on earth. My husband, Ben, turned to me and said that Miss Ruth will be the "Bill Gates" of heaven. He's always thought very highly of her and regards her life as one spent entirely in deep devotion to her Lord. He imagines that she will have loads of treasure in heaven because of it.

Evelyn Hinds

It has been a joy for me to meet and fellowship with Evelyn Hinds. Evelyn found her life's work portraying Corrie Ten Boom in a "one-woman drama." I have been greatly blessed as I have listened to her excellent presentation. In her home, she has a great collection of books about Corrie that she has studied. Corrie has become like a spiritual grandmother to Evelyn through these books.

Evelyn Hinds Writes

I heard about and read about Miss Ruth for a year before I got the chance to meet her. Even after our phone introduction, it took another several weeks to get a meeting scheduled into her busy life. She was eighty-three years old, and I was in awe already.

As Miss Ruth has told me stories and answered questions for me over this past year, she has taught me to have a great love for Jewish people. In years past, I have not had much contact with Jewish people. I felt inadequate and not sure of just how to relate. When I learned that she started with little knowledge, I was encouraged. I could see how God had given her the love and knowledge she needed, and surely God would equip me.

Miss Ruth has shushed some of my murmurings and complaints with her often-said, "All that matters is doing the will of God each day!" My husband and I have adopted that saying to remind us of that glorious truth. It's one of our favorite sayings to toss back and forth to each other when things are muddled or seemingly off-track.

Miss Ruth's stories and experiences have become part of my life. This friendship we share as we serve God is truly one of God's great blessings to me.

Doug Williams Writes

I am a United States Active Army Chaplain with the 554 Engineer Battalion stationed at Fort Leonard Wood, Missouri. A year ago, I returned from deployment in support of Operation Iraqi Freedom.

Doug Williams

I previously served a church in the Dallas area. It was at this church that I met a woman who characterized one of the strongest faiths I have ever seen. She was like a dear grandmother but at the same time would laugh at my jokes like someone my age. I am in my thirties. She had a tremendous love for God's Word and loved to teach it to young children. It was at this point in my life that I felt I had failed and would never find the opportunity of serving God. Without going into tremendous detail, I was at the end of my rope. I felt very discouraged about circumstances and really did not have a high view of myself or my future.

When God called me out of my wilderness to be an Army Chaplain, I had a hard adjustment to make. It took time to believe in myself again. I loved to preach God's Word but had not done it on a regular basis for some time. As part of the application process, I was required to write an essay for the interviewers. Going through the interview process seemed overwhelming, and I desperately needed someone who believed in me to encourage me. Ruth Wardell was that person, and I will never forget her strong, firm voice telling me that what I had written would never do. She made me change everything.

I joined the Army, went to the Army Chaplain School in Fort Jackson, South Carolina, and have gone on to serve God in the military. It is the best thing that has ever happened to me. I give God the praise and honor for making this happen, but I will always be grateful for his love and support through His servant, Ruth Wardell. I believe that because of her support I am doing what I am doing today.   CH (CPT) Doug Williams, Battalion Chaplain

February 2008 Reunion

In February of 2008, we had a three-day reunion of the group of Jewish believing children that I taught in New York City back in the 1950s and 1960s. These young people are now in their fifties and sixties. They came from Boise, Chicago, Philadelphia, California, Atlanta, and Israel. Many of them had kept in contact sporadically, but some had not seen each other for thirty to forty years. They had a glorious time of. They came together as if they had never

February 2008 Reunion

been apart. As I watched them interact, I could see the years being peeled back to the 1950s and 1960s when they first became friends. They were beyond excitement to be together.

They shared what had transpired in their lives since the last time they had seen each other. They also expressed their joy in the Lord. I had not seen some of them for forty years. It warmed my heart to see and hear how they were still walking close to Jesus after all of these years and doing the will of God. I felt that what I had taught them as far as staying in the will of God for their life's work had manifested itself in each of their lives. It was a joy to me. Many of them had grown in the Lord. Some had become missionaries and pastors. That's the best gift a student can give any teacher.

Additional Thoughts

I never married and do not have any close family ties. I don't have any natural sons and daughters, which in most families look out for your welfare and best interest. But, even so, it has served as a great motivator for me. It's immensely intriguing to watch and see how God, my Heavenly Father, who is faithfully taking care of me now, will also take care of me in the years to come.

Writing a book about one's life brings back a flood of memories. Most of the memories shared here were good memories. God, in His mercy, favored me with many awesome times in life.

However, life is not always easy, and there were many times when people were very unkind, sometimes very critical of what was done. I often said that you could sit in your house, and do your job for the Lord and find yourself in a lot of trouble because critical people seemed to need to gossip about you and say really bad things about what you were doing. If you are in ministry for the Lord, you will have troubles, because one of the biggest things Satan would like to do is to get you discouraged so that you will quit. There were times when I thought these thoughts. However, the Lord would always remind me of His calling and give me the grace to carry on and complete the tasks that He had for me to do.

Now, at the age of eighty-six, I am still doing ministry work. Each week, six of us gather together to learn how to be disciplers. We call ourselves the "DD's"—the Dedicated Disciplers. We are using Arnold Fruchtenbaum's material called *Come and See*. All six of us are being wonderfully blessed and enjoying learning all the new things that Arnold presents. Each one takes a turn at teaching the materials, so we are also learning to become good teachers. We have also become good friends and prayer partners. It remains to be seen just what the Lord will do as we reach out to new women to help them become discipled.

**Ruth and the
Dedicated Disciplers**

I teach Bar/Bat Mitzvah lessons every other week to four dear Jewish children. A friend comes once a week for Bible study. I call the retirees from the Chosen People Ministries each month, and many folks call, and we share the Word together. So I am still busy. It seems to me that we need to be doing the Lord's work until the day He calls us home.

As you all know, getting older is not really the "Golden Age." It is difficult to decline physically and to lose all of your friends. Even since Jeff Gutterman and I started to write this story, several of those we are writing about have gone to Heaven. However, even as we lose our long-time friends, the Lord gives us new ones to minister to and share joy with. The Dedicated Disciplers are a good example of this. Also, as you get older, you know that soon you will have the blessing of seeing your friends again. Praise the Lord.

In the writing of this book, over and over again it was very inspiring and fantastic to realize how God has graciously led me day by day and year by year to follow His awesome plan that He has lovingly made for me.

My prayer is that each of you will experience the great JOY that comes from following the plan of God for your life. Romans 12:1–2 says: "I beseech you therefore brethren, by the mercies of God that you present your bodies a living sacrifice, holy, acceptable to God, which is your reasonable service. And do not be conformed to this world, but be ye transformed by the renewing of your mind, that you may prove what is that GOOD and ACCEPTABLE, and PERFECT will of God."

May our passion in life be to do the will of God until He takes us home.

POETRY

My Father's Poem

My father wrote a poem for me, on my 21st birthday. It was titled: "To the Best Girl in the World."

To the Best Girl in the World

There was a girl named Ruthie
Who grew so very fast
That dresses would not fit her.
They often were half mast.

But now she's twenty-one
And will be able to vote.
No longer is she little
But now a lady of note.

Her life has been most happy
For her Savior she makes known
And many little children
Have heard of a heavenly home.

Her future will be blessed
As she does the will of God
And someday in the glory
The golden streets will trod.

Shoes have also been a problem
So we give her a pair today

And hope she'll have good understanding
In all her earthly ways.

An Ode to Ruth Wardell

By Naomi Seidman

Ruth calls me her mother-in-law,
Now how can this thing be,
Since she is turning eighty,
And I am only sixty-three?

The answer's in the Bible,
God's Book of endless truth,
You see, my name's Naomi,
While hers, of course, is Ruth.

Ruth was my camp counselor,
At a place called Sar Shalom.
My very first time away,
From family and from home.

I was feeling kind of frightened,
Also sort of glum.

Then Ruth called me "mother-in-law,"
And she became my chum.

With Ruth at my table,
There was laughter, there was cheer,
So I realized all at once,
I had nothing more to fear.

She played a cool accordion
And sang along to boot.
For a camp counselor,
She was really quite a hoot!

Through the years, we've kept in touch.
Once lived in towns next door.
Bible class was at her home,
Taught by best friend Eleanor.

I had two small children then,
Who Ruth would watch for me.
While I sat and learned of Jesus,
They were safe upstairs, you see.

Then we moved to California,
And she came that way too.
She even taught my children,
Of Messiah's love
so true

Now she lives in Texas
And we in Oregon.
Once she traveled here to see us,
And boy, did we have fun!

We took her on a jet boat ride

Along the River wild.
The wind was strong, it blew her hair,
And gave it a new style.

The noblest thing about her,
That I've very much adored,
Is the way she always shares
Her great love for the Lord.

Her devotion continues,
Though she's getting "long in tooth."
And that's the reason why
She's called "Ruth with the truth."

She gives out His Word
To the young and to the old,
As she teaches of Jesus,
His love she does unfold.

Her spiritual children,
Span four generations,
So today she is honored,
With loving admiration.

She deserves many kudos,
Hugs, kisses and thanks,
Even some gratitude
For her witty little pranks.

So Happy Birthday to Ruth,
My dear "daughter-in-law."
You've had eighty blessed years,
Hope you have many more.

To Our Dear Miss Ruth

By Carol Betten

I wrote this poem for a party given for Ruth a number of years ago to celebrate her fifty years of ministry:

You may think all angels are in Heaven,
But you would not be right.
There's one right here in this room
With us this very night.

She has blond hair and a loving face
And a heart of purest gold.
Gleaming eyes and a mischievous smile
Which she's earned, or so we're told!

She loves our kids with all her heart
You can tell by all she does.
She listens, she laughs, she teaches, she sings,
But most of all she loves.

She give them presents, teaches them songs,
They find her very kind.
They always miss her when she's gone
And when she's here, they try hard to mind.

And to the "grown ups" in our group
She also is a friend.
An example, an encourager, a mentor, a mother
Loyal to the end.

A woman of faith, a "Godly Gal"
Who encourages us with her faith.
She's loved the Lord through thick and thin,
You can see it in her face.

She shares the gospel and God's love,
Those who listen are very smart.
She knows how to share a word of truth
That speaks right to the heart.

"Be strong in the Lord" I remember she's said
Often to inspire.
She models this every day of her life,
Even when she's very tired.

For 50 years she's served the Lord,
She's faced all the children fearlessly.
The verse "Suffer the little children to come unto me"
She's taken very seriously.

She's impacted many, many people
Yes, many lives she's touched.
And in case you can't tell just yet,
We all love her very much!

Yes there's an angel in this room right now,
With us all tonight,
And if you've guessed it's Ruth Wardell
Then you'd be oh, so right!

A Lady Named Ruth

By Jackie Hager

It's not just her gift of teaching.
It's not just her love of the truth
Nor her history with missions
Or her eagle-eyed vision
Or the way we all call her "Miss Ruth."

It's partly her positive outlook,
Partly her love for fun.
It's the way she knows the Good Book
And the life she lives in the Son.

It's the way she loves the children.
It's the time she spends to prepare.

It's the strength she has in her 80s
And the effectiveness of her prayers.

She's a beacon of joy.
She's a well of giving.
She's our greatest GOY—
And she's still proving
That life can be sweet no matter what stage
If we learn how to walk
And focus our gaze
On the ONE called YESHUA, the source of all truth . . .

The ONE who sent us our precious Miss Ruth.

CPSIA information can be obtained
at www.ICGtesting.com
Printed in the USA
FFOW01n2332291017
41588FF